POSITIVE BUSINESS

the secrets of
SUCCESSFUL
SELLING

POSITIVE BUSINESS

the secrets of
SUCCESSFUL
SELLING

KRISTINA SUSAC

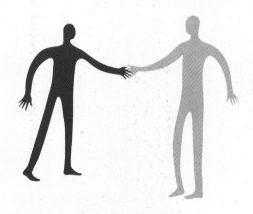

DUNCAN BAIRD PUBLISHERS
LONDON

The Secrets of Successful Selling
Kristina Susac

First published in the United Kingdom and Ireland in 2004 by
Duncan Baird Publishers Ltd
Sixth Floor
Castle House
75-76 Wells Street
London W1T 3QH

Conceived, created and designed by Duncan Baird Publishers.

Copyright © Duncan Baird Publishers 2004
Text copyright © Kristina Susac 2004
Commissioned artwork copyright © Duncan Baird Publishers 2004

The right of Kristina Susac to be identified as the Author of this
text has been asserted in accordance with the Copyright, Designs and
Patents Act of 1988.

All rights reserved. No part of this publication may be reproduced or utilized in
any form or by any means electronic or mechanical, including photocopying,
recording, or by any information storage and retrieval system now known or
hereafter invented, without the prior written permission of the Publisher.

Managing Editor: Julia Charles
Editor: Louise Bostock
Managing Designer: Dan Sturges
Commissioned artwork: Melvyn Evans and Ken Orvidas

British Library Cataloguing-in-Publication Data:
A CIP record for this book is available from the British Library.

ISBN: 1-84483-046-2

10 9 8 7 6 5 4 3 2 1

Typeset in Bembo
Colour reproduction by Colourscan, Singapore
Printed in Singapore by Imago

This, my first book, is dedicated to the two most significant women in my life.

My mama, Janja. Thank you for always putting your family first, and providing Nick, John and me with the happiest, and most loving childhood; and for teaching us to always have faith. Volim Te!

And to my little daughter Natalia Janja, my light and inspiration.

CONTENTS

AUTHOR'S INTRODUCTION

Why do some people excel in selling products and services and creating partnerships, while others who work just as hard fall short of meeting goals and quotas? Does the star salesperson have better product or market knowledge, more experience perhaps, or better technique, plain and simple?

In today's ultra-competitive marketplace, skillful selling is no longer enough. Today's buyers know that they can demand more than ever as part of the purchasing process. They are bombarded on a daily basis with offers from selling companies, so when a salesperson offers more than the product at the lowest price, buyers sit up and take notice.

Consultative Partnership Selling is my approach to selling. It offers not just the right product/service, the right price and the right delivery schedule, but also a long-term business partnership in which the salesperson understands the changing needs of the buying company, and works as a partner to fulfill those needs in a continuing relationship. Consultative Partnership Selling can never by definition be an aggressive or manipulative technique because at its heart lies the necessity to work together to create a mutually beneficial outcome.

This book is an introduction to the core selling skills, with an emphasis on those special skills that comprise the Consultative Partnership Selling approach. Chapter by chapter, you will learn how to research your territory and get to know the players in it, how to work smart, directing resources toward activities that you know will bring results. It shows you how to approach new prospects with confidence and

how to lay the foundations for a firm, long-term relationship. It has advice for the hard tasks in selling, tasks that most salespeople will tell you they care little for: cold-calling, giving group presentations, chosing the moment to close, handling buyer objections. Chapter two looks at important skills such as asking the right questions, understanding body language, and improving communication skills. Chapter four is devoted to how to survive the selling profession: how to integrate your career with other aspects of your life; what to do when things are not going your way; and how continuously to review and improve your own performance over the years.

Carefully and consistently applied, with practice and with experience, the Consultative Partnership Selling approach could be the start of your biggest success yet.

chapter 1

PREPARING TO SELL

Nothing lends itself better to selling success than preparation. Indeed one of the most common reasons for failure to make the quota is a lack of strong, sensible preparation and planning. Preparation shows you who is a good prospect and who is not. It tells you how to approach your customer and what you can expect from a meeting with him. It makes you appear more knowledgeable, trustworthy, and credible in his eyes. Regular planning and preparation keep you on track with your sales quota and give you early signs if you need to change course.

This chapter looks at the skills required at the very start of the selling process: research, organization, prioritization. It shows how to define and manage your territory, how to plan and organize your time. It also tackles two of the biggest fears for many salespeople: generating new leads and cold-calling.

It provides some very useful practical advice for increasing effectiveness in these important activities.

The chapter ends by looking at how to plan your sales appointment, including how to formulate effective questions and how to qualify the prospect.

ARE SALESPEOPLE BORN OR MADE?

Perhaps you've been pondering whether to pursue a career as a sales professional, or you are a sales professional looking to refine your style and improve your success rate. In either case, you will probably at some stage have asked yourself, "What exactly is required, and do I have what it takes?" "Are women better suited to the job than men?" "Are only gregarious, out-going personalities likely to be successful?" There are no meaningful answers to these questions. A specific profile of a successful salesperson does not exist. Successful salespeople come from a variety of backgrounds, and correspond to an array of personalities. But there are several common qualities, which can pre-determine your likelihood of success.

The most important personal characteristics required are tenacity and a strong desire to win. At the same time successful salespeople are good at setting goals and working to them. It is also important that you have a realistic idea of your own style and goals in the context of the company you are working with. If your organization is customer-driven, dynamic, and constantly changing, and you are not, then there is a good chance that dissatisfaction will develop on both sides.

Selling is particularly well-suited to the person who is self-motivated, self-directed, and self-managed. Your employer provides the sales targets, and you are responsible for determining the most effective way to exceed them. You should also be a strong communicator, and be open and receptive to new ideas. You should have an analytical mind, because you will need to be constantly assessing customers, situations, problems, solutions, and opportunities.

As a sales professional, it is important to think of yourself as a member of a "helping" profession. Remember that you are a teacher, innovator, and time-saver. An effective sales professional knows his customers, their industries, their applications; is a customer advocate, team player, and problem solver; and is constantly adapting to meet the needs of his clients.

The skills required of successful salespeople today are different from those of yesterday. Whatever got you here today is not enough to keep you a top performer tomorrow. The ability to be constantly changing both your style and methods to suit the expectations of today's environment is a must.

KNOWING YOUR PRODUCTS

Product knowledge is one of the most important assets a salesperson can possess. Clients prefer to purchase products and services from those who know what they are selling, and who fully understand the product's uses. Without product knowledge, other selling skills are useless.

Becoming familiar with your product means: understanding its applications; knowing who uses the product; its features and benefits; your company's position in the market; what differentiates your product from competing products; and knowing how to demonstrate your product confidently.

The traditional way of gaining product knowledge is through employee training programs, and by reading product manuals. But corporate literature is often written by technical experts who tend to focus on the technical details of the product, rather than on the intricacies of the heart and mind. While it is important to be acquainted with the features of the product, you will need more than this. Products sell not only on what they are physically, but also on the hope they represent to the buyer. Your product may have a dozen technical advantages, but unless you can demonstrate that these represent some sort of solution to the customer, remove a stress, or address a problem he is facing, you will not succeed. People buy good feelings and solutions to problems.

Gaining and maintaining this kind of product knowledge is accomplished first by asking yourself honest questions about your product line, in terms of how it can be most usefully applied by your client in his need to solve problems. Do this by stepping into the customer's shoes. Ask yourself why

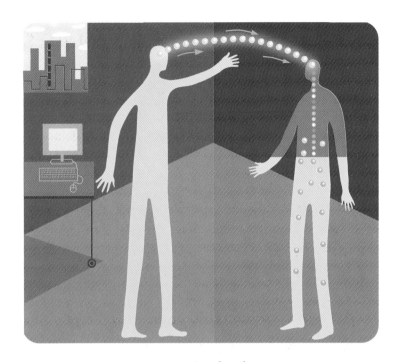

your top customers remain loyal to your company. Understand what your organization does well, and how it is differentiated from its competitors. Think about which customers have recently left your organization and what motivated them to do so. Were the causes for defection a result of pricing, service, product quality, or technical reasons?

A good source of information on customer attitudes to the product can be co-workers, particularly in customer service, who collect input directly from your clients. Your customers themselves will also be likely to give suggestions on how their future needs can be met: important feedback not only for you but also for your colleagues in R&D.

To optimize your ability to relate to your clients, and the products and services they are using with your organization, ideally, you yourself should be using them. Put yourself in your customers' shoes; experience the product first hand.

KNOWING YOUR MARKET

Once you have a strong lead on a prospect, it's natural to want to jump right in to the active selling process. But resist the temptation to forge ahead until you've done the necessary information-gathering. Researching the full background to your customer's market segment and overall requirements will give you a general picture of his activities and therefore of his needs. When you finally meet your prospect face-to-face, you will appear well-informed, and this will put you in a positive light – you have understood the prospect's needs. This, after all, is your primary function as a potential partner.

There are many ways to learn about the businesses in your territory and the industry in general. The Internet is perhaps the most useful tool for research. Corporate websites can provide all sorts of company information, and industry-

specific newsletters can keep you up to date with the latest trends, statistics, and information. You will also glean information from business newspapers and magazines, and your company may have a clippings service for this purpose. Join the industry's association – important for networking and for intelligence-gathering.

Make use also of the knowledge of existing customers. Given the opportunity most business people are happy to talk about their company, its positioning in the marketplace, and its competitors, plans, and strategies. This information is invaluable. The way to get yourself on your prospect's agenda is to find out what the agenda is.

WORK SOLUTION 1

Planning a User Group

User Groups are groups of key existing customers brought together to provide feedback to the selling company. Meeting usually on a semi-annual basis, User Groups can be a mine of information about evolving industry trends and changes, and market demands. A side-benefit to forming a User Group is that it gives your key customers a sense of belonging, they feel they are part of your company and that you value their feedback. When a User Group member is contacted by a competitor, he is far less likely to entertain their proposal, because he has formed a personal relationship with your company. Take the following steps to set up a successful User Group.

1. Decide on your goals/objectives. What feedback and ideas would you like to explore in the session with your key customers? Decide how you will evaluate the success of the meeting internally.

2. Decide who should attend. Think about which clients are bringing in the most revenue, and which have the greatest potential to do so in the future. Who is most likely to contribute with depth and breadth? Whose presence might inhibit the free contributions of others?

3. Design an agenda and coordinate it with your overall marketing strategy. Consider covering "hot points" related to the product or service to challenge or verify internal thinking. Be sure to consider legal and ethical questions when soliciting your customers' advice. There could be industry, regulatory, or company standards to use as guidelines.

4. Practical details: find a suitable venue; determine how long the meeting should last and whether it should take place on a work day or on a weekend; determine what incentives you could offer (golf, concert, theatre, free products, etc.).

PLANNING YOUR TERRITORY

The word "territory" can be used in different ways. It can be defined as a limited geographic area, a specific market segment (hospitals, government, retail, etc.), an existing customer base, a list of top 50 prospects, or a combination of these and other definitions. Whatever your territory your purpose in planning it is the same: to put in place a plan that will allow you to familiarize yourself with the customers – potential or existing – that reside within your territory, and to marshal your resources to achieve maximum account penetration.

The first step in planning your territory is to determine your sales objectives; and these will stem from your sales quota. Define your objectives in terms of necessary and measurable activities, and in terms of results.

For brand new business, measurable activities can be listed as: number of phone calls made, number of businesses

TAKE OWNERSHIP OF YOUR TERRITORY

A useful perspective I like to share with my students is to think of your territory as your own personal business franchise. It is yours to nurture and to grow. Take ownership of your territory – feel yourself to be wholly responsible for it. View yourself as a "fixture" and as a neighbor within your territory. If you do others will see you in this light too. It will give both your new prospects and your exisiting clients a sense of security when they realize you are "in your territory" on a regular basis, learning about the different businesses that are situated within it, and staying up-to-date with their needs and concerns. Taking ownership means that you can put your creative talents to good use. Be constantly thinking of new ways to make your personal business as profitable and productive as you can.

canvassed, number of appointments set, number of account needs analyses carried out, number of presentations made, and number of accounts closed. Don't forget the existing business in your territory and, when looking at measurable activity, include the number of visits to existing accounts.

Results can be measured in terms of revenue growth, market-share growth, account retention, account product expansion, customer satisfaction, and customer referrals. The more satisfied your customers are, the more likely you are to retain them, and the more likely they are to tell others about you. Make customer satisfaction a central part of your territory-planning. It will enhance your measurable results.

An essential part of your territory-planning includes forecasting the revenue potential of the accounts within it. Establish these estimates by researching your prospects' business volume, or using factors specific to your product and industry. Once you have an idea of the potential volume, classify each prospect according to potential and work them accordingly. Keep in mind that 80 percent of your business revenue will likely come from 20 percent of your clients.

MANAGING YOUR TERRITORY

Once you have a territory plan in place, ensure its success by actively managing it. Territory management is related to time-management. Knowledge and time are great assets, and how well you allocate them is meaningful to your success.

Working smart and leaving little to chance requires planning the next day's work the evening before. Avoid falling into the bad habit of deciding what to do only after arriving at your office. The key is to plan and to be proactive, rather than continually reacting to emergencies, which will inevitably occur when you fail to manage your territory. Planning tomorrow at the end of today allows you first of all to review the day's progress while it is fresh in your mind. It also draws a line under the day's work, leaving you to have a relaxed evening knowing that you are as well-prepared as you can be for what tomorrow may bring. Primed by your planning session, your brain will be working as you sleep, and

MANAGING YOUR KNOWLEDGE

Knowledge management is crucial if you are to run your territory effectively. By tracking the results of each call you make, you will avoid repeating actions unnecessarily, and when you make follow-up calls, you will not be wasting time by asking questions already answered.

For each prospect you meet with, regardless of their present level of interest, make a Prospect Profile Form. This form should have space for the following information: account name and address and other contact details; names and positions of key management members; type of business the company specializes in. Include information acquired when you were learning about your market. You will also need space to note the source of the lead: did you find the lead when canvassing? cold-calling? through a referral? from an advertising campaign? This information is useful when reviewing the most effective methods for lead-generation. Most importantly, make sure you have a space to note action points and follow-ups, with dates.

often you will wake up with solutions and ideas already planted in your mind.

When planning your day, just listing the name and number of the people you need to call is insufficient. Each call must have a stated objective beside it to keep you focused on your goal. I always like to mix types of calls – existing customers with new prospects – balancing the more difficult cold calls with the more pleasurable calls to customers I know and like.

Minimize traveling time between meetings by visiting as many existing customers and new prospects as possible within one geographic area at one time. For example, avoid going out to one appointment in the morning and returning to the exact same area in the afternoon. Poor scheduling of appointments can mean many wasted selling hours. If this situation is unavoidable, use the "between time" to canvass your territory. Prospecting for new customers needs to be a continual process.

Make each call as complete as possible by being fully prepared. Check that you have everything you need to avoid having to return to deliver something you should have had with you in the first place. After each call make notes of future action required. Does the prospect need references, a presentation, or perhaps even a trial of your product? Always follow up your visit with a brief note of thanks, conveying your appreciation for your prospect's time and input.

PREPARING A SALES KIT

As you begin to lay the groundwork for visiting potential new customers, think about all the tools you can assemble to help you present your products and services in an informative, exciting, and illustrative light. Take this sales kit with you whenever you go to an appointment with a prospect or an existing customer. While many companies are switching to sales presentations in electronic formats, others still prefer the traditional, print-based interpersonal approach. It is best, perhaps, to have both styles available, and to decide which to use based on the customer's preference.

Envision your sales kit as your tool for educating your prospect on the benefits of using your service. Put yourself in his place, and think about all the things you would need to

know about the product/service in order to feel confident about buying and using it yourself.

When considering the content of your sales kit, keep in mind that we are attracted by visual stimulus. So, make your sales kit as visually appealing as possible. Logo- and theme-consistency, as well as high-quality paper and printing, texture, and design convey messages to your clients that your company has a clear identity and is serious. If you are selling a non-tangible, a service perhaps, the visuals you include in your sales kit are all the more important, because your prospects cannot touch and feel whatever it is you may be selling. They need to imagine it, and you need to do everything you can to help them with their visualization.

In putting together your sales kit, keep all of the esthetic and visual factors at the forefront of your mind, and make sure you include: marketing information produced by your company which gives information about its background and a company description; a list of the benefits the prospect can glean from using your product/service; press releases relating to your product/service; letters from happy customers; a list of frequently asked questions and their answers; pricing information; verifiable relevant statistics/graphs that illustrate how your company or product can be differentiated from competitors; videos or CDs you can leave with the customer to view at leisure.

Being prepared, well informed, and informative enhances your credibility, and your success. An up-to-date and accessible sales kit assists you every time in being just that.

MANAGING YOUR SALES QUOTA

In sales a quota is used to measure your productivity. All the work activities you undertake, planning, presenting, and follow-up, are ideally designed by you, with the ultimate goal being to meet or exceed revenue expectations. Your quota is what drives your activity, and only you can control and take responsibility for your performance.

Checking your course of action and continually evaluating the way you do things will ensure that you get to where you need to go. Just as a pilot never flies without checking his instrumentation and his flight path so that he stays on course, so must you as a salesperson. This requires not only keeping your target in your sights, but also being able to measure your performance, day by day.

Start by looking at the sales quota established by your company and what meeting it means to you personally in financial terms. If you are happy with the income you would receive by simply meeting your quota, fine. If you have a larger income requirement, however, you will need to adjust

WORKING TOGETHER

The beauty of being in the selling profession is that it allows for a great deal of autonomy: in general you get to decide how best to organize your activities. However, personal support is invaluable. Some companies operate extremely supportive structures, typically with weekly sales meetings during which team members share success stories and discuss problems. Sales teams can also work together to help individual members develop new strategies for meeting their quotas. If you are self-employed or working in a one-man team, you have several options to help with support and motivation, ranging from listening to motivational tapes, to joining community and industry organizations that may put you in touch with other self-employed people.

your level of activity accordingly.

How high your weekly, monthly, or quarterly sales quota is set will be related to the selling cycle – the length of time it takes to make a sale from start to finish. The more complicated the sale is, the longer the selling cycle. For example, it is likely to take longer to get to a "Yes" in a situation that involves multiple locations and several layers of decision-making than if you are selling to the sole owner of a small family business. Once you know the length of the selling cycle, you will be able to set daily and weekly targets to ensure that there is a regular flow of accounts coming to fruition.

Think about the specific tasks that are required in the sales process: canvassing, cold-calling, referral-seeking, calls to the existing customer base, contact with decision-makers, face-to-face presentations, proposal-planning, and closing. Create daily, weekly, and monthly progress reviews and reports to gauge your productivity, checking it against your quota. How many people did you call? How many appointments with decision-makers? What is the estimated revenue potential of your prospects? Are you on target with your goals? If not, what actions can you take to get back on track?

Selling is as stimulating as it is challenging. You will succeed by having a realistic goal, and by frequently checking where you are in relation to that goal.

PROSPECTING

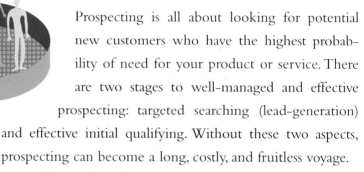

Prospecting is all about looking for potential new customers who have the highest probability of need for your product or service. There are two stages to well-managed and effective prospecting: targeted searching (lead-generation) and effective initial qualifying. Without these two aspects, prospecting can become a long, costly, and fruitless voyage.

Building a list of prospects is a never-ending process and is very important to your success. Unless you have a steady flow of new names, you will soon be out of sales leads. Many salespeople often resort to the following, which can provide basic lists of companies quickly: professional groups and organizations; directories for trade shows; commercial lists; new business license registration lists; telephone books; business directories; newspaper ads; on-line marketing; databases. Of course, your company may also supply initial sales leads from such activities as direct-mail campaigns or by purchasing mailing lists on your behalf.

Calling every name on a list, however, may turn out to be time-consuming and costly; only a few of the leads may actually qualify for your product. Prospecting on a more personal level can sometimes be more successful. Here are some key prospecting methods:

• Personal networking. Join a community organization that will put you in touch with all sorts of people from all walks of life. Some may turn out to be well-qualified buyers.

• Public speaking. Take every opportunity to raise your own profile by speaking about some aspect of your business.

WORK SOLUTION 2

Building a prospect pipeline

The following exercise graphically illustrates that both the company sales team must constantly be prospecting in order to ensure an on-going flow of new customers. It can also serve to help set personal targets and organize activity on a daily, weekly, and monthly basis.

1. On a large writing pad, draw a picture of an inverted triangle, or a funnel.

2. Now divide the funnel into four sections.

3. In the uppermost quadrant of the funnel, write "100 possible customers." In the quadrant below this, write "50 prospects." In the next quadrant below that, write "25 presentations," and in the lowest and smallest quadrant, write "12 sales."

4. This prospect pipeline is based on the principle that you will need to call on two "suspects" before you land a "prospect." (A suspect is an unqualified potential customer who has expressed an interest in your product, or anyone who appears to have a need for it. Suspects become prospects once you have qualified them and they seem to have a genuine need and ability to purchase the product.) Different industries have different ratios. For example, perhaps you will need to look at 200 suspects to generate 50 prospects.

5. If you are new to your industry or to selling, ask colleagues what they feel the standard ratios are, then re-draw the prospect pipeline showing the new proportions. Use these ratios to fix your own personal targets, and plan your activity accordingly across the timeline of your particular selling cycle.

Follow up talks by meeting members of your audience, distributing company literature, and collecting business cards.

• Referrals from existing customers. Ask satisfied clients for names of friends and colleagues whom they feel could also benefit from your product/service.

• Canvassing your territory. When you are on the road, visit new office buildings. Ask the receptionist for the name of the relevant decision-maker. Leave your company literature with the receptionist; along with a brief note to the decision-maker, telling him or her you will be getting in touch shortly.

• Find out who are your competitors' customers. Now there's an excellent opportunity for fresh leads!

• Stay in touch with existing customers. Be the one to tell them of new products and be the first to know about changes in their requirements.

Whoever is not your customer remains a prospect. Change is constant. Maybe tomorrow there will be a new decision-maker who will be open to your products and services, if the one you are calling on today is not.

The next step is to qualify each sales lead. Qualifying is the process of finding out whether your lead or "suspect" is a "prospect" and therefore worth the time and expense it takes to pursue. Qualifying takes place throughout the sales process as you find out more and more about the company you are selling to. At this very early stage, it prevents wasting time and effort calling on unsuitable leads.

When prospecting the salesperson is looking for potential new customers who have the highest probability of need for their product or service. Some other factors in determining a good prospect are: type of business, accessibility, ability to pay, and company income. Does the prospect have a want or need for your service? Does he have the authority to buy, or is he an influencer in the final buying decision? Is the final decision made within your territory or in another branch office? Most importantly, does the prospect have the ability to pay for your goods/services? A new customer who does not pay their invoices will not advance your cause!

Continual prospecting coupled with effective early qualifying maximizes results, minimizes wasted time, and increases the morale of the sales force through higher hit ratios.

COLD-CALLING

We salespeople love the challenge our jobs represent, we love being with our clients, and the "high" we get from discovering and meeting their needs, but the one aspect of our jobs we perhaps least enjoy is looking for new leads and making cold calls. The reality is that the joy of making the sale could not occur without the proper groundwork. Selling is a numbers game, and the more leads we generate, the more prospects we have, and more prospects mean more sales!

Simply put, cold-calling is the act of getting in touch with potential new customers who do not know you and are not expecting your call. The two methods of cold-calling are on the telephone and face-to-face. When embarking upon this type of prospecting, it is important that you have a positive attitude, and relate to it as a way of creating and maximizing your sales opportunities. The more cold-calling you do, the more lucrative your profession will be.

The biggest commodity you have in sales is time, and the biggest mistake is wasting it. Before starting to make those calls, put your sales leads into categories that are likely to maximize success. At the start of my sales career as a general business account representative for Sprint, I had a monthly quota of $10,000 in new-account revenue generation. At the time Sprint was selling only long-distance phone service. It was up to me to determine which types of businesses were most likely to do a lot of long-distance calling, and to organize my time accordingly. I realized I would be wasting my time calling on any business whose client base was entirely local. Instead I decided to call on manufacturing companies,

shipping companies, banks, distribution companies, telemarketing firms; companies that common sense told me do a lot of long-distance calling.

When sorting through your lead list, attempt to prioritize in terms of geography, revenue potential, and product potential. Plan to call your top revenue potential prospects first, as it may take a little longer to secure an appointment.

Make sure you set aside an hour or two daily for cold-calling. Calling during "normal" business hours is not always the best way to go, as often key decision-makers start work early in the morning, and stay later into the evening. Your chances of reaching your decision-maker increase if your calling hours reflect his working hours.

Before you pick up the phone, think about the ways your product/service could be a potential fit for him, and keep in

mind that you only have a minute or so to make the call. Don't forget, your goal is to secure an appointment. With your hand on the phone, check that you are in a positive frame of mind, and that your facial expression reflects this. Surprisingly, the look on your face can often be "heard" on the phone.

One of the biggest challenges in cold-calling is getting past the receptionist. Always be sincere and enthusiastic. Arrogance and sneakiness are readily identifiable, and are not recommended. Never lie to an administrative worker, trying to pass yourself off as a friend. If the administrator tells you the boss is busy, unavailable, or not interested at this time, politely ask if you may get in touch at a later date. Make politeness your hallmark, and keep in touch.

If you are cold-calling in person (make sure you are professionally attired), introduce yourself, explain to the receptionist that you were just meeting with another client in your territory, or familiarizing yourself with businesses in your area, and would appreciate the opportunity to introduce yourself to your contact person. If the person is available, be brief, respect their time, and request an appointment for a future date, unless of course he happens to be available to meet at that moment. If your contact is not available, leave some literature behind and follow up the next day.

Cold-calling is a necessary evil for most salespeople, but with a positive attitude and plenty of practice, some salespeople master the art, and benefit greatly from their success.

WORK SOLUTION 3

Positive cold-calling

The best way to ensure that you always have someone new to present to is by keeping your activity level high. Nothing serves to better enforce this goal than cold-calling. It is ironic that the activity that is most likely to ensure your success is one of the most dreaded! Creating and maintaining a positive attitude toward this activity will make cold-calling work for you. This checklist could help you help yourself.

1. **Put yourself in a positive frame of mind** by reminding yourself that cold calling is an activity that allows you to serve as a conduit in helping others. When you are out in the field looking for new prospects you are putting yourself in a position to help someone by introducing him to a product/service that will in some way improve conditions for him.

2. **Remember that face-to-face contact is valued** in an increasingly depersonalized world. It reinforces the fact that you take your job seriously, and care enough about your clients to take the time to get to know them personally.

3. **Be realistic**. Do not set yourself up for disappointment by expecting every business you call on to be enthusiastic about your visit or your call. It is normal to have to contact numerous businesses before you encounter one that is a good fit. Remain positive just the same, because people are attracted to those who have a positive countenance and appear to be enjoying themselves.

4. **Reward yourself** at the end of each cold-calling day, regardless of how many appointments or presentations you made. When you know you will be doing something you enjoy once you have completed your canvassing, you are more likely to do it with a positive approach.

CALLING FOR THE APPOINTMENT

The first step in making cold-calling work for you is understanding that every call is an opportunity to find out something about your territory and to meet a possible prospect. With this attitude firmly fixed in your mind, it is necessary to review the actual content of each call and the manner in which you make it.

Unsolicited or unexpected phone calls are often bothersome to a senior executive, yet without the initial contact, how would your organization get in the door? The manner in which you make the call should set you apart from your competitors. The most important thing to remember when calling your prospect is to think about all the various ways your product or service can meet his needs. Are you calling

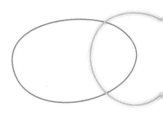

to introduce him to a product that will make life easier? Enhance his company image? Save him time and money? Streamline efficiencies? Is what you are calling to offer going to "help" the company? If the answer to any of these questions is "Yes" (and if you have done your initial qualifying properly, it should be), the reason for your call can be seen as quite legitimate.

Many salespeople begin the telephone conversation with "I'm sorry to bother you." Do you really think a stranger will want to make an appointment with someone who is "bothering" him? When you do something to help someone make his business more successful or his life less stressful, do you apologize? Of course not! So don't apologize for calling your potential customers! You must be enthusiastic about all the benefits your client can glean from your product. You must be excited about introducing the prospect to a new and

ENJOY YOURSELF

Try to enjoy yourself when calling your prospects. And don't get discouraged if someone does not immediately agree to an appointment. I can recall phoning the Chief of Technology for a large food manufacturer over some months. He was always very friendly, but somehow would never agree to an appointment. I started thinking about what I could do to stand out from the other salespeople calling him. I decided to express mail him one of my shoes, along with the note: "Dear Mr Smith, I'm just trying to get my foot in the door." I needed to drive over to pick up my shoe, and as long as I was going to be there, he agreed to meet with me! My shoe captured his attention, and he became curious to meet me. The results were very productive. The creative approach is risky, and you must be confident that your creativity is appropriate. As I had already had numerous phone conversations with this prospect, and we had a certain rapport, I was pretty sure my humor would be appreciated.

better way of doing business. Let the enthusiasm come through in your voice.

The next important thing to remember when you are requesting a meeting with a prospect is to word your question in a way that convinces the client he can say "Yes." Most salespeople make the mistake of asking, "Can we have an appointment?" which invites the prospect to say "Call me in two days (two weeks, two months)," or "Fax me your company literature." Instead, try personalizing the following script when calling for an appointment:

"Good day. This is (*your name*) with (*your company name*). I'd very much like to set up an appointment with you to demonstrate how (*your company*)'s products and services can enhance your company's image, improve efficiencies, and save you valuable time and money. I'm going to be in your area next Tuesday and Friday, and would appreciate 20 minutes of your time. Which day looks best for you?"

This script, when used in a confident and competent manner, accomplishes two main things. First, it immediately tells the prospect what they can expect from investing 20 minutes of their time with you. You are going to introduce them to a new/better product/service. This service will benefit them in that it will enhance their image, save time or money, and improve efficiencies. Who can say "No" to this? Second, people like choices. In requesting the appointment, use the Alternate Choice Technique. "Which day is better, Tuesday or Friday?" You are directing the prospect to look at his calendar, find time for you, and agree to a meeting.

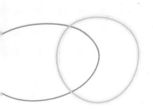

WORK SOLUTION 4

The alternate choice technique

Using a question that suggests two equally desirable answers, both of which confirm that your prospect is moving ahead in the discussion, is known as the alternate choice technique. If in place of asking an alternate choice question, you ask one that suggests a "Yes" or "No" answer, your prospect is more likely to choose "No." Everyone thinks it is easier and safer to say "No" than it is to say "Yes." After all, "No" is among the first words we learn as children. The sales professional uses the alternate choice technique to avoid asking questions that put "No" into the prospect's vocabulary.

Form an alternate choice question using the following steps:

1. Ask yourself what are the positive and negative answers to your question?

2. Select the positive answers that are most likely to benefit you.

3. Based on your selected answers, formulate the question so that either potential response advances your cause.

Try the alternate choice technique at home. Next time you want Johnny to wash the dishes, think about your request. "Johnny, will you wash the dishes?" is likely to be met with "I have to do my homework," or "I don't feel good". Try reformulating your question as: "Johnny, were you planning on washing the dishes now, or an hour from now?" Now Johnny has no option but to choose one or other of the alternatives. Again, if your partner generally prefers to stay home for dinner and you would like to go out, try reformulating your question: "Do you prefer to go out tonight for a Mexican or Italian dinner?" The important point, that you go out for dinner, is a given, so either answer works for you!

PRE-CALL PLANNING

Perhaps the most dangerous habit an account manager can fall into, is visiting a customer without having a pre-set goal or strategy in place. You need to determine exactly what it is you expect from your sales call, otherwise you can't possibly engage the prospect in the most effective and purposeful manner and you will have lost a valuable opportunity. I have accompanied hundreds of account managers all over the world on their sales calls, and have observed that the biggest disservice they make to themselves is to just "show up and play it by ear." Doing so makes the prospect feel unimportant, and the account manager comes across as an amateur. There are two elements here. You must, of course, know your product/service inside out, but as the buyer's sophistication

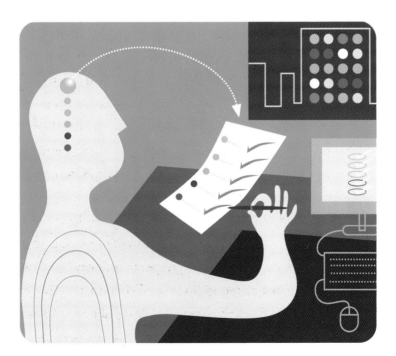

and knowledge of available market choices increase, so will his demands and expectations. A prospective client expects you to know about your product and service offering, but how much do you know about his business sector? How experienced, knowledgeable, and trustworthy are you as a prospective business partner? Second, you need to have a clear idea of what you wish to gain from the meeting – without a goal in mind it is likely that you will come away with nothing.

We have covered ways of acquiring information about your industry and about specific players in your territory in previous sections. Before making your visit, it is wise to review the information you have gathered, and consider how you might use it to your best advantage. For example, an event involving one of your prospect's competitors may be in the news. Or perhaps there have been recent regulatory changes, and you can ask how these changes might affect your client's business. Perhaps your prospect has just moved to the area (ask how he is settling in) or has just expanded into your field (ask for the thinking behind the decision to do so). Mentioning such matters will increase your standing in the eyes of your prospect, and will go a long way toward earning his trust and eventually his business partnership.

The second element in pre-call planning – determining your desired outcome – is just as important as making yourself knowledgeable about your prospect's industry and business. It is wise not to set up a single, all-important objective as your goal, particularly when thinking about your first meeting with the client. Experienced salespeople put a

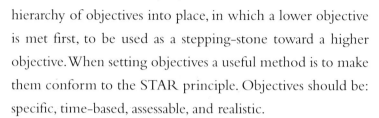

hierarchy of objectives into place, in which a lower objective is met first, to be used as a stepping-stone toward a higher objective. When setting objectives a useful method is to make them conform to the STAR principle. Objectives should be: specific, time-based, assessable, and realistic.

Specific All objectives can be defined in terms of quantity. Think in terms of how much product/service the prospect may need.

Time-based Objectives must be stipulated in time. Within what time frame do you plan to get the information you need so that you can help your prospect meet his business objectives?

Assessable Your objectives need to be measurable. What will you use as your benchmark? Specific revenue figures often work best!

Realistic Be careful not to demotivate yourself by setting unrealistic objectives. Salespeople should not expect a sale every time, and need to remember always to have alternative goals in place if Plan A does not work. This can be as simple as asking for permission to stay in touch with the prospect in case their needs change. Remember to set a primary goal, a secondary goal, and an alternative.

Planning goals for your appointment has several major advantages. First, it allows you to focus, and this enables you to set the stage for the prospect, and better guide the dialogue. Second, strong pre-call planning minimizes stress. As you have done your account planning, you will appear more experienced and feel more confident.

WORK SOLUTION 5

Creating a pre-call planning worksheet

Systematizing your pre-call planning is useful – it saves time and helps to direct your thinking in preparation for your appointment. Create a template worksheet using the STAR headings for your objectives: specific, time-based, assessable, and realistic. Make careful notes under each heading and use them in conjunction with the information you have gathered about your prospect's industry and his business.

Specific

Ask yourself, "What do I want to achieve from this visit?" Have specific

objectives in mind. What is the information you are trying to gather?

For example, perhaps you are trying to verify your prospect's need for your

product. Alternatively you may be at a stage where you might ask for the order.

Time-based

How soon can you get the information you need to help you address the client's

concern/problem? What is the average sales cycle for a client of this size?

Assessable

Think in terms of the steps required in the process of making this sale: the

tasks that are involved in the sales process in the company you're selling to,

as well as the internal goals of your company. How will you meld the two?

Realistic

Once you've determined how you want to approach the account, strategize your

visit by having an optimum goal in place, as well as a couple of back-up options

so that you maintain a reason for continuing to stay in touch with the client until

you are able to meet his needs.

QUALIFYING

In day-to-day purchasing decisions, we all go through a process of evaluation, a checklist of sorts, asking ourselves various questions before we decide if we want to buy something. Some of the things we ask ourselves include: "Do I want this?" "Do I need this?" "Can I afford it?" "How soon should I make the purchase?" When you are evaluating your prospects and their account potential, you are making similar determinations. This process is known as "qualifying." Some of the main determinations you need to uncover before proceeding too far into the sales process include: "Does the prospect have a need?" "Does he want the product?" "Does he have the authority to make the purchase?" "Does he have the ability to pay?" Your skill in asking the right people the appropriate questions enables you to decide if there is a potential fit between your company and the prospect.

When qualifying a prospect, successful salespeople are looking at the following aspects: need, authority to buy, ability to buy, and timescale.

First, it is important to identify whether or not the customer has a need for your product/service. If your prospect already has your competitor's product that can be a very good sign, because at least that means he has a basic need. Once you determine he has a basic need, you can further probe and ask what his expectations would be of your product, to see how you might be able to meet his needs. Perhaps the prospect is unhappy with his current supplier. In this case he has an unmet need that your product could supply. Perhaps the prospect has an ongoing problem with staff turnover, and

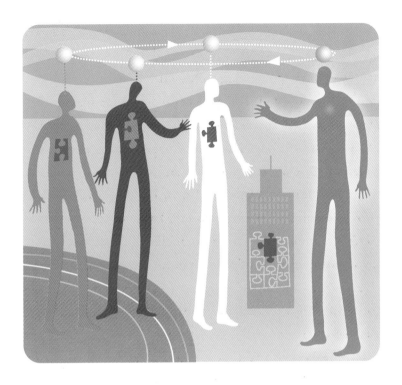

your service could help him meet the need to better retain staff. This qualifies him as a prospect.

Sometimes a prospect has a need, but does not want the product badly enough to justify costs, internal analysis, and other procedural purchasing requirements. Conversely, I've found myself in situations where a prospect has called me requesting a specific technical application of my product line (a "want"), and upon further probing and analysis, I learned he did not actually have a need for the product. Asking the right questions helps to make sure you are doing what is best for the prospect, that you are fulfilling a real need.

Making certain your prospect has the authority to buy your product or service is another essential qualifying question. For example, many salespeople find themselves well into the selling process only to learn the prospect cannot buy because he is locked into a three-year contract with another supplier. Ask questions about where the final decisions are made – and who makes them. Whenever you believe you have located the decision-maker, verify your understanding. There may be more than one decision-maker. If you are told that others are consulted in the final decision-making process, ask to include those people in your future meetings.

Third, it is vital to make sure your prospect has the budget and ability to pay for your products and services. Is there money already earmarked in the prospect's budget for your product/service? Does the company actually have funds to pay your invoice? When I was researching my hot prospects' credit backgrounds, I was surprised to learn how many multinational companies have very poor credit histories, or are very slow to pay.

Finally, asking questions about the prospect's decision-making time frame is very relevant to how you allocate your own time moving forward with your prospect. If your prospect needs your product next week, but you have a two-month delivery interval, you may have an obstacle. If your prospect has two years to make his final purchasing decision, you will need to reassess the overall account potential, and how much time you should be spending on it today.

The most successful salespeople are skilled at asking the right qualifying questions, and doing so will help you identify strong prospects, clarify your expectations of them, and reduce objections later in the process.

WORK SOLUTION 6

Asking qualifying questions

The ability to successfully qualify a prospect is one of the biggest time-savers you can acquire in the selling profession. Often you may get several of the answers you require by asking just one question. Make sure you ask the prospect what he likes about the way his needs are currently being met, and this includes asking what he likes about his present supplier. Don't just focus on the prospect's dislikes. The following steps include some sample qualifying questions that you can adapt to help guide you in the process.

1. Determine need

"How are you fulfilling this requirement for (*your product*) at present?"

2. Determine want

"What would you like this product/service to do for you?"

3. Determine ability to pay

"Is there money allocated in the budget for this project?"

"Are you locked into any pre-existing agreements?"

4. Determine time frame

"When would you like to see this project completed?"

5. Determine the decision-maker

"Are there any other individuals you consult in

making your final decision about this product?"

6. Determine where purchasing decisions are made

"Is the purchasing decision made at this office or elsewhere?"

chapter 2

THE ART OF COMMUNICATION

One of the most exciting realities of being in sales is that it provides opportunities to interact with a vast array of different people. Communication could be said to lie at the very heart of selling as a profession, and it is crucial that salespeople learn how to communicate in a skillful and meaningful way.

Our main mode of communicating is speech, and learning to control and enhance the way we speak and what we say can lead to success in a wide variety of circumstances. But non-verbal communication is just as potent in relaying messages, and far more difficult to harness to our own ends. At the same time different people communicate in different ways, and being able to "package" your message to best suit each individual's style means the difference between an average performer and a star.

Communication is used to build rapport with the prospect, to learn about his needs and to unearth information that might lead to matching a need to a product. Asking the right questions and actively listening to the answers is key to building trust and to finding out about the prospect and his business needs.

DEVELOPING RAPPORT

Rapport is used to describe a harmonious and trusting relationship between people. Rapport between the salesperson and the prospect begins from the moment contact is made, and should grow through the sales process. When you have achieved rapport with your client, he is more relaxed and forthcoming, and more likely to discuss his company and its needs. Consequently, you are able to speak to his needs and offer workable solutions. Buying is an emotional decision which we later justify through the use of reason and logic. If the client feels that with you he is in a safe environment, he will look for ways to be in agreement with your proposal.

Rapport is created through a combination of four elements: positive body language, respectful behavior, keen

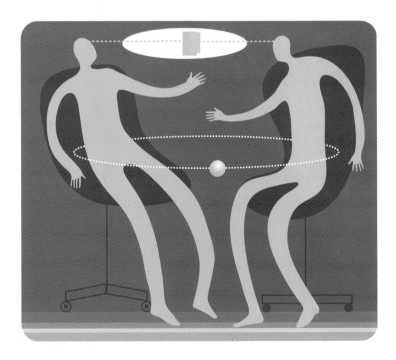

listening skills, and credibility. Your body is a powerful tool for non-verbal communication. You can use it to create rapport by showing the prospective customer that he has your full attention. Keep your eyes on the customer's face. Take special care not to be checking the clock, gazing at the floor, looking out of the window or at other people. At the same time remember your posture. Hunched posture conveys fatigue and disinterestedness. Sit up and square your shoulders to show that you are alert and interested in your prospect.

Respect for your prospect is conveyed in numerous ways, but most importantly in the way you introduce yourself. Keep it formal and use his title and surname until he gives you permission to be more informal. By the same token do not enter a person's office and do not sit down until invited to do so. Avoid presenting yourself in an overly familiar way until the prospect has given you the appropriate cues. Remember that in non-American cultures, the business environment is often more formal.

We have two ears and one mouth, and we should use them proportionately. Attentive listening is a crucial aspect of rapport-building. By listening carefully you communicate that you care about the prospect's opinions and needs. At the same time listening is your primary tool for information-gathering – you cannot meet your customer's needs without knowing and understanding what they are. Sometimes salespeople may intend to listen, but they are so worried about some other element of the meeting that what the client is saying does not sink in. Make special effort to clear your mind of distractions, and allow this time to be a worry-free zone. Don't forget to make notes of the main points, and if you are on the phone, tell your prospect that this is what you are doing to explain any pauses in the conversation.

A good way to keep your relationship moving steadily along is to provide a general framework for your current conversation and to indicate what the future process might be. Make sure you have an agenda for your meeting, and that you share it with your prospect. Ask him if he is happy with it; if any key points that may be important to him 'are missing. This will show that you are respectful of the prospect's time and his ideas and input. Before you leave a meeting, go back over follow-up actions you may have discussed, leaving your prospect with a sense of agreement.

Strong relationships are based on shared experiences and mutual understanding. But how is it possible to develop a rapport with everyone? You may think that you and your prospect are like two fish from different seas, with very little in common. But keep in mind that you both reside in water, you both swim, and you both fear the larger fish! Similarly, it is possible to find some basis of commonality with almost anyone. People who are very different in temperament, background, and interests can find value in each other and work well together. Being authentic and feeling comfortable when you are in the presence of your prospect goes a long way toward enhancing rapport.

WORK SOLUTION 7

Laying the foundations for good rapport

A trusting and open business relationship starts from the moment the salesperson first meets the prospect. But launching straight into business can make it seem as if you are not really interested in your customer as a person. Spending some time in small talk can break the ice and establish a firm connection from the outset. The following practical steps can be used to get you through those first few awkward moments.

1. Arrive at the meeting a few minutes early. Compose yourself, ready to present yourself in a relaxed, comfortable, and focused manner.

2. Use direct eye contact and a warm smile when greeting the client, and extend a firm handshake. This will demonstrate to the client your warmth and sincerity.

3. After the introductions follow in a natural way into your friendly, non-business dialogue by making reference to potential common interests. Look around the office for clues as to what his interests might be: photographs of children, sport trophies, pictures of places. Ask: "Are these your children?" "Is this your vacation home?" "What sport did you win this at?" The office may be particularly modern, or it may have an interesting view. Comment on this.

4. Listen to what the customer is saying. You will enhance your credibility by demonstrating your eagerness to listen and adapt to the conversation, rather than attempting to stick to a pre-set personal agenda.

5. Be responsive to the customer's body language. If they are not engaging, move on to the purpose of your meeting by summarizing the main points you would like it to cover, and asking, "Does that sound OK to you?" Being in agreement is a good starting point for developing rapport.

MEETING YOUR CUSTOMER'S PERSONAL NEEDS

One of the key skills in Consultative Partnership Selling is understanding the customer's needs so that a solution can be found through your product or service. Customers generally make positive buying decisions when their needs are fulfilled on three levels: personal, organizational, and professional.

We all have all six primary needs within us, but one or two usually dominate.

• The achievement-driven type of person often does several things at once. He wants you to hurry up and state your case because he has many things to do. Be concise; get to the point.

• Recognition-motivated types may have diplomas, certificates, awards, and trophies on display. Try to find a sincere way to comment or show an interest in his accomplishments.

• The person with a need for order is likely to be very systematic. Offer him as much detailed information as you can; be punctual and organized.

• Demonstrate to the power-oriented prospect how your proposal can enhance his already highly regarded reputation.

• The customer with a need for security avoids risks and resists change. Give him comparisons that illustrate how your product will make him feel even more secure.

• Be ready to spend extra time with the client with a need for belonging. Invite him out to lunch or to a company function. This type is a great team player and hates to make decisions alone, so ask if there are others you can involve in your discussions.

WORK SOLUTION 8

Expanding your capabilities

Understanding the varying needs of your propsects and customers is the key to meeting them. It is easy to relate to customers whose personal needs are similar to ours, but it is a greater challenge to succeed with those with whom we seemingly have less in common. The following exercise will help minimize barriers between you and your customers by assisting you in a personal inventory, which will allow you to expand your ability to understand a greater variety of customer needs.

1. On a piece of paper, list the six major personal needs: achievement, recognition, order, power, safety, belonging. Nominate which two you feel figure most dominantly as your primary personal needs.

2. With respect to your two most dominant needs, list the characteristics of your behavior (your attitude, the things you say and do) that you feel define each of these personal needs.

3. Next, think about a specific customer who has a dominant personal need that you have difficulty meeting. List all of the behaviors that this person exhibits and that define his dominant personal needs. Compare your dominant behaviors with those of the customer whose personal needs you find challenging to meet.

4. List all of the activities or approaches you could conceivably take with the customer to minimize the barriers between the two of you.

Put yourself in your customer's shoes in this way whenever you come across someone you find hard to reach, or who exhibits personal needs that are very different from your own, then change your behavior accordingly, and observe how much more receptive your prospect becomes.

MEETING YOUR CUSTOMER'S ORGANIZATIONAL AND PROFESSIONAL NEEDS

Now that we've explored meeting the personal needs of the customer, we're ready to look at how we can meet the needs of his organization and those of the prospect in his professional role rather than as an individual.

Be aware that your customer may be considering several different organizational needs and inter-departmental purchasing criteria in making his final buying decision. Very often the range of needs contrasts quite markedly from department to department, and your customer may be wrestling with how to satisfy all these needs with a single proposal. The range of buying considerations that exist in

most larger organizations include, for example: Financial, operational and administrative, and sometimes a single solution may need to satisfy both internal and external customers.

Financial considerations generally center on how your solution might impact revenues, how much investment it may require, and how soon there may be a return on that investment. Operational and technical considerations relate to how your solution will improve operations, and how it can be implemented without disrupting production. Needless to say, there will be many questions of technical compatibility. Administrators will want to know how your service will impact the company's employees, perhaps enhancing employee productivity or motivation levels. Might it perhaps lead to a reduction in or expansion of the workforce? Finally, most large businesses today seek to satisfy not only their external customers, but also colleagues ("customers") from other departments who are also users of the solution.

As well as trying to meet the needs of his organization, your customer will always be looking for ways to meet his own professional needs, which are loosely defined as his on-the-job requirements and responsibilities. These requirements are determined by his role in the company. He will be thinking about how your service can perhaps simplify his job, give him greater visibility, or help him achieve advancement.

The sophisticated salesperson, who can appeal to the personal, professional, and organizational needs of his customer will create a win–win sales climate. The customer looks good to his employers and you make the sale!

PRESENTING IMMEDIATE
BENEFITS STATEMENTS

As soon as you have a basic idea of the personal, professional, and organizational needs of your prospect, it is important
to turn this knowledge to use. To secure your customer's
attention, focus his thinking, and create an interest, you need
to make it clear to him how he may be able to benefit or gain
from your company's offering. Successful salespeople do this
by introducing their product with a very general "Immediate
Benefits Statement."

Benefits can be divided into two groups: emotional and
logical. Emotional benefits appeal to one's sense of image,
prestige, popularity, and security. Logical benefits, on the
other hand, include such examples as increasing revenue, saving time or money, gaining a competitive advantage, or
improving safety.

Right at the outset you must present your product/serv-
ice in terms of both the emotional and the logical benefits
that the client stands to gain. You will need to decide whether
to present your product primarily in terms of emotional or
logical benefits, and how you decide depends upon your customer's personality type and his role. For example, a person
from a financial or technical background might respond
more strongly to logical benefits, while a person in an administrative role might respond better to an emphasis on
emotional benefits. It's a good idea to always present your
product in terms of both categories of benefit, but it is your
skill as a salesperson that determines which category will
dominate your initial presentation.

The Immediate Benefits Statement should be made within the first few moments of the presentation. Of course, with as yet only a general knowledge of the customer's business, it is not possible to be too specific. The most common statement draws together a number of generalities regarding your company's previous experience with the product/service. The following is typical: "Working as we do with several companies like yours, we have found a range of benefits from using our service. All our customers have found significant increases in revenue after installing the system and a number report a decline in customer complaints." After a statement like this, you will probably have your customer's full attention. He has some idea of what he has to gain from answering your questions, and is probably keen to know more.

FACT-FINDING: MAKING THE DIAGNOSIS

In Consultative Partnership Selling, the aim is to develop a mutually beneficial relationship based on trustful cooperation. However, before such a relationship can develop, you as the salesperson need to find out where the customer needs help. Customers buy solutions to business problems, and your selling strategy should be focussed on problem-resolution. The fact-finding phase of the first interview with a prospective customer is aimed at finding out where the customer needs the kind of help that you can supply.

In this step it is useful to think of yourself as a physician. Just like a good physician, the successful salesperson will

probe for information and conduct a thorough exam about current problems (pains, or "where it hurts") before presenting the "cure." Too often less experienced salespeople fail to ask about the customer's needs. They assume that they know what the customer wants, presuming to tell him what would be best for his company. Envision walking into a doctor's office, holding your head in your hands. Before you can say a word, the doctor begins to tell you how he can help you without so much as asking, "What appears to be the problem?" Just as you would not trust a physician who writes a prescription without asking about your symptoms, you wouldn't trust a salesperson who leaps into a recommendation without first learning about your company needs! Think of yourself as a doctor. You are visiting a customer (making a house call) to get to know the organization (the patient). Ask questions! Look for the illness. What is the company presently doing that could be done in a more efficient way?

Every "ailment" your customer experiences is an opportunity for you to relieve the pain. Your job is to figure out where the buyer is hurting. With each illness you are able to alleviate, the buyer will see you as a valuable resource, and you will be on your way to developing and consolidating your relationship and increasing your sales. So what types of pain relief should you be probing for?

A prospect has great cause for concern if he senses diminishing revenues, customer allegiance, customer satisfaction, product quality, market share, employee productivity and morale, or profit to name a few. Pain is also felt when a customer senses an increase in staff turnover, labor costs, operations/facilities-management cost, and competition.

Ask such questions as: What is the size of the company? what are their present growth plans (so that you can anticipate changing demands)? Who are their present suppliers? What do they like about their present suppliers? How could the product currently in use be improved?

Once customers feel comfortable with you, they will begin to speak more freely about their needs, and you must remember to encourage their flow. At the fact-finding stage, the customer should be doing 80 percent of the talking, and the salesperson 20 percent. Be very careful not to answer your own questions. If you begin substituting your thoughts and opinions for those of the customer, you will run into problems as the sales process evolves. When you fall into the bad habit of answering your own questions, you are permitting the customer to not make you aware of a potential objection or need he may have, and you are diminishing the opportunity to uncover his genuine needs.

By identifying the unique needs of each potential customer, you will quickly and cost-effectively match the right buyers to the right product or service. A diagnostic, consultative partnership approach to selling, presented in a non-manipulative way, distinguishes a prepared salesperson from the rest of the competition. The account manager who can prove he understands his clients' needs develops long-term relationships with a larger network of partners, resulting in larger market share.

WORK SOLUTION 9

Understand the illness before prescribing a remedy

The better you can understand your client's business problems, the more able you will be to develop a solution that suits his purpose, and thus build a long-term relationship. Your path to understanding is paved by asking questions, listening to the answers, and synthesizing the information. This exercise focuses on the types of questions you will need to ask in order to maximize your knowledge of the customer's requirements.

1. Ask the prospect for an "industry overview." Relate your question to something you already know about his sector and get him to elaborate. Ask him questions such as, "Thinking about trends in your industry at the moment, would you say you expect your business to be growing in the near future?"

2. Once you have an industry overview, get him to be specific about his company's overall operations with regard to size, number of physical locations, employees, etc.

3. Next, try to learn a little about which product/service the prospect is presently using in place of yours. Ask what the primary factors were in selecting the competitor's product/service.

4. Upon learning the factors that motivated purchases of competing products, ask the customer to tell you what has worked well with them, as well as what improvements or enhancements he thinks could be made to them.

5. Use the above types of questions in your fact-finding phase so that when you come back for your next appointment you can present potential solutions in terms of the customer's actual needs.

QUESTIONING TECHNIQUES

In terms of fact-finding, your questioning skills are your number-one asset. Questions will serve as road maps, which enable you to guide the conversation in the appropriate direction. Remembering what to ask is far more important than remembering what to say.

Questions are tools that can be helpful only if you know how and when to use them. They are used to qualify a potential buyer, determine his attitude about existing vendors and products currently in use, and understand his predisposition toward you, your company and your product/service offering. Questions also allow you to uncover detailed, factual information about your prospect's potential buying motives. Use your questions to form alliances with your prospects by honing in on the benefits they will glean as a result of working together.

Why are questions your most powerful tools for success? They work like magic because they require you to focus on your prospect, not your own company or your product. They make your prospect feel important because they provide an opportunity for self-disclosure, and when you show a sincere interest in him, your prospect feels valued and cared for. At the next meeting you will be able to build on this by showing that you have learned from the answers he gave and have given his particular situation careful thought.

Be certain to make the questioning stage a natural part of your conversation so that it does not appear to be an interrogation. Think of yourself as a partner/consultant rather than as a cross-examiner.

WORK SOLUTION 10

Practical questioning techniques

Asking questions encourages dialogue between you and your prospect, and dialogue produces trust, the very foundation of your sales efforts. The following techniques for asking questions are extremely useful in the fact-finding phase of the sales process.

1. Try organizing your questions in such a way as to maximize your understanding of the prospect's goals by classifying them using the Past, Present, and Future technique. This will allow you to understand why they made the decisions they did in the past, what they currently require to fulfill their needs, as well as how they perceive their future requirements.

2. Preface your fact-finding stage with a general introduction to put the customer at ease: "In order clearly to understand your preferences and learn more about your company, I'd like to ask you some questions about your needs and expectations ..."

3. Begin by asking broad, general questions, and then gradually make your questions more specific.

4. Avoid "closed" questions, requiring simple "Yes" or "No" answers, except in the latter part of your conversation to confirm existing information.

5. Make use of "layered" questions to prompt more specific answers. For example, you may ask, "How do you see your company six months from now?" The client may offer a general response such as "We see ourselves as number one." You may layer the question by asking, "Could you please describe to me what number one means to you?"

NON-VERBAL COMMUNICATION

Non-verbal messages are expressed through our appearance, the way we dress, our facial expressions, gestures, eye-contact, the way we hold our head, and the way we carry our body. It is estimated that as many as 80 percent of the messages we communicate to each other are sent using this form of communication. For you to maximize your credibility and power with the buyer your words need to match your body language and your tone. In the event of a mismatch, your buyer will disregard the words, and focus on the non-verbals.

Our clients begin making assumptions about our credibility from the moment we walk into the room, long before we have the chance to prove ourselves professionally. Such assumptions are often based on the way we dress. You can be well-educated and highly experienced, but if your attire does not conform to your credentials, the latter are automatically diminished. Happily, though, dress and grooming are the easiest aspects of our non-verbal communication to correct.

The way you choose to dress should not distract from your message, and it should actively contribute to the perception you want to create. Successful salespeople have what I call "presence." Presence refers to the aura, authority, poise, and dignity a person establishes in the company of others. Avoid dressing in a flashy or overly trendy way. There is nothing as guaranteed to communicate reliability as a well-tailored, well-fitting, understated suit. Buy the best quality you can afford. Your clothing should be clean, neatly pressed, color-coordinated, and appropriately accessorized. It goes without saying that you should also be well-groomed.

But what about the body inside the suit? Be aware as much as possible of the messages you are continuously transmitting through your facial expressions, gestures, and head movements. A furrowed brow conveys confusion, nodding the head up and down communicates agreement, and a side-to-side movement of the head indicates disagreement. An erect posture communicates confidence, and a smile communicates agreement, or a shared interest or experience.

Very often we are not aware of the nervous movements we make – gestures that tell the customer we are uncomfortable, impatient to leave, or nervous. Examples are pen-clicking, jangling with keys or change in our pockets, or playing with our hair, earrings, tie clip, etc. An effective way to uncover whether or not you are making unconscious movements that might detract from your central message is to video-tape yourself during a mock presentation with a

HOW NOT TO DRESS FOR CREDIBILITY

While conducting a customer-service seminar recently for a client in Moscow, my students told me that during the previous session the trainer's subject had been the importance of the first impression. The focus of her presentation was the message that in the first few seconds of a meeting, the "audience" makes an instant decision about you and your credibility based on the way you look. The students told me that they immediately disregarded her information because of the way she presented herself. They said that she was advising them on how to improve their appearance, but she herself was overly made up, wore a suit that was a size or two too small for her body, with a skirt that was not flattering. Additionally, the roots of her hair were very dark, and the ends were all bleached out. In short a disaster to her credibility! Although the presenter may have had some very good advice to share, the audience was not open to it. Perception is often more powerful than reality!

colleague. The discovery of our own unconscious gestures can have an enormous impact!

Of all the features on your face, none is more expressive than the eyes. It is vital to make immediate eye-contact with your prospect: if you focus on him you will communicate warmth, enthusiasm, and caring. Do not allow your eyes to wander. If you dislike what you are doing, are ill-prepared, or are nervous, this will be reflected through your eyes. The beauty of eye-contact is that it works both ways. While your prospect is able to read your messages, you will also be able to see how he is feeling. If he is confused by what you are saying, or disinterested, you will immediately see this and will be able to clarify or redirect the conversation to other topics.

WORK SOLUTION 11

Communicating positively without saying anything

Eighty percent of our interpersonal communication comes in a non-verbal form: The expressions on our faces, our willingness to make eye-contact, and our head movements, hand gestures, body posture. Of all of them eye-contact is the most powerful tool for developing an open and trusting relationship with the customer. Follow these steps to evaluate your eye-contact and to gain an understanding of the value of eye-contact when trying to develop rapport.

1. Start by asking yourself questions about how you make eye-contact. Are you aware of where you are looking when you are talking to another person? Where do you look when you are listening? Where do you look when you look away?

2. Enlist the help of a couple of colleagues: One will play the role of your prospect, and the other will sit beside the two of you and observe your dialogue. The observer should provide you with feedback on the duration of your eye-contact and what he observed you doing with your eyes. For best effect your first eye contact should be a steady 15 seconds.

3. Start again, but this time, your colleague begins by making steady eye-contact with you as you talk to him. He then looks away from you for no less than 20 seconds before returning his eyes to your face. Later in the conversation, your colleague should try to look anywhere but at you as you continue talking.

4. At the end of the exercise, tell your colleague how you feel. Do you feel valued and interesting or do you feel disregarded and "shut out."

5. Reverse roles, allowing your colleague first the benefit of your undivided attention, conveyed through steady eye-contact, and then gradually allowing your eyes to wander. Compare your experiences.

VERBAL AND VOCAL COMMUNICATION SKILLS

Although the greatest initial impact is made through non-verbal communication, verbal language, and the way you deliver it, is essential to the overall picture. Why is this so? The effective use of words can give you leading-edge results, by getting your message across in a persuasive and memorable way. Your skilled use of language distinguishes you as a well-educated and interesting person, both qualities we tend to trust in others.

In order to be understood by your prospect, common associations need to be connected to your words to maximize effectiveness and understanding. You need to make your words dynamic, accurate, and appropriate for the listener.

Dynamic language is active, clear, and illustrative: Paint a picture with your words. Metaphors and analogies are great tools in achieving this.

Accuracy is essential in eliminating misunderstandings. When you are comfortable with a subject, it is easy to assume that everyone in the audience knows what you are talking about. Choose your words carefully. Use examples to strengthen your meaning.

Appropriateness means tailoring your language for the person or people who will be hearing it. Use words your prospect will understand. If he is not from within your industry, avoid acronyms and jargon with which he may not be familiar. Use inclusive personal pronouns such as "you," "we," "us," which form a link between you and the listener. Try to speak about facts, opinions, and experiences that relate to

circumstances your listeners will recognise. Make your language correspond to the knowledge level of your listeners and their level of sophistication.

Now that we have touched upon the importance of words, we need to look at how to make your message stick in the mind of the prospect. You can achieve this with your vocals – the way in which you say your words. Vocals include such characteristics as the quality of your voice, articulation, pitch, rate, and volume. All of these influence how your buyer perceives your attitude, emphasis, and emotion.

Variety is the key to holding your listeners' attention. Just as movement catches people's attention, so do changes in your voice. Avoid speaking in a monotone. You cannot be persuasive if your buyer is falling asleep! Use intonation by

changing the tone of your voice while you are talking, and laying particular emphasis on key points.

Ensure that you articulate your words clearly. Pronounce all of the syllables of each word, and say each word completely. Slow down if you have to.

Adjust your volume so that it is comfortable for the audience, topic, and situation. If by nature you have a quiet voice, getting your message across in a group meeting may be difficult. Conversely, an overly loud voice may make you seem overbearing and bullying in a one-on-one situation.

As the body grows older, the natural tone, or pitch, of the voice deepens, and so we tend to associate a lower voice with maturity and experience. In contrast higher-pitched voices are associated with youth and excitability, perhaps not the kind of qualities a salesperson wants to convey. Changing the pitch of your voice is very difficult to do with any consistency, and should not be attempted, but if you know that when nervous, startled or excited the pitch of your voice rises, try to stay in control at those moments.

Inflection involves adding variety to your tone. Use inflection to emphasize key points, and to move from one idea to the next. Your listeners need the aural cues that inflection provides in order quickly to grasp what you are saying.

If you feel that your voice is letting you down (for example, perhaps it is naturally quiet) consider seeking out a voice coach, who can help to improve your vocals. You may also want to invest in a single coaching session that would cover these issues if you are planning an important presentation.

WORK SOLUTION 12

Polish up your vocals

Make your voice work for you in catching and maintaining the attention of your audience. Here are some practice exercises to help you make your voice more resonant and effective.

1. Read two sentences from a newspaper article in a conversational tone.

2. Inhale deeply through your nose. Your diaphragm should flatten downward, pushing the abdomen out, and then your chest expands. Keep the shoulders still.

3. In your mind picture a group of listeners sitting in rows. Now exhale while repeating your test sentences. Imagine that your voice can be heard 12 to 15 rows beyond your final row of imaginary listeners.

4. Make sure your breath supports your voice – that you do not run out of breath, ending up with a squeak. Use your diaphragm to control the flow of air. Ensure that the sound is not being pushed from your throat.

5. Practice your pacing while reading a newspaper article. Modify your delivery speed. Make longer and shorter pauses. Listen to yourself all the time.

6. Consider your pitch while performing the same exercise. Say certain sentences in a high sing-song fashion and experiment with a range of tones.

7. It is impossible to know what we really sound like to other people. To find out record yourself running through these exercises, evaluate your own performance and then repeat.

RELATING TO BUYER PERSONALITY TYPES

One aspect that makes selling particularly fascinating is the fact that you are constantly interacting with a variety of personalities. It is easy to sell to people who are similar in nature to you, but it is an art to know how to relate to the others. The first step is to be aware of the various personality types, and the second is to know how to adapt or "flex" so that you reach each one. The four primary personality types are: Authoritative, Analytical, Influencer, and Relational.

The Authoritative type has a leadership personality, likes to be in charge, and prefers talking to listening. He will want to control the agenda. He is strong and ambitious, and a fast thinker. He tends to draw conclusions quickly and dislikes indecision. He can be a risk-taker. Offer him choices – he

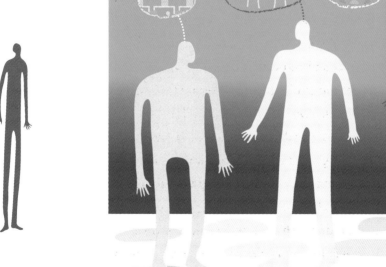

does not like to feel limited. Get to the point. He often has only two questions on his mind: "How much will it cost?" and "How soon can I have it?"

This personality type is the strongest of all four and strength admires strength. Make sure you are attentive, active, and assertive. It is important that you are strong, but take special care not to be dominant. This personality type will shoot out his questions and he'll expect you to know the answers.

The Analytical type is known as the hard worker, the data collector, and is respected for the fact that he plays by the rules, and is extremely well-organized. He is task oriented, and prefers to work alone, rather than on a team. For this reason, he is rather remote in the workplace. The Analytical type takes his time making decisions, and would not dream of doing so without thorough analysis of all the data. This type values precision — and likes exact answers, not estimates. He does not accept the spoken word and likes everything in writing. The Analytical type is cautious, not a risk-taker.

Prepare an agenda and send it to him in advance of the meeting. He will want to study it and be prepared. Make sure you are prepared as well. Avoid small talk and do not be too personal. Be prepared to spend as much time as he needs and do not hurry him along. When presenting provide sufficient data, begin at the beginning, and go step by step, making sure everything has a logical flow. Focus your presentation on ways your service can diminish risks and alleviate problems — for example, by explaining post-sales service support and all of the guarantees you are able to offer.

Influencer types, on the other hand, are always interested in learning about the latest innovations and tend to be instinctive and impulsive. They are superb communicators and present themselves as confident, assertive, and open to new information, which is an excellent opportunity for you. Align yourself with the Influencer by matching his speed, style, and openness. Influencers are in tune with their emotions and those of others, and are aware that the decisions they make impact others within the company. You can assist them in appealing to this need by demonstrating to them how your product is of a reliable quality, and by emphasizing the high level of satisfaction attributed to its use.

However, the Influencer is the quickest to experience post-sale remorse. Loyalty may be an issue with this buyer, as he relies heavily on instinct. As readily as he arrived at his decision to go with your product, he may be just as apt to change his mind. Be prepared to work hard to maintain this relationship post-sale.

The fourth personality is the Relational type. This is the people person, the team player. This personality type is the best communicator of all, particularly in reading non-verbal communication. Change makes him uncomfortable and therefore he makes decisions slowly. To maximize success with the Relational type, be patient, and be willing to spend a little more time. He builds trust and rapport based on positive personal feelings, so share personal information with him. Focus your presentation on one or two product details that most interest him. Do not overwhelm him with excessive detail.

WORK SOLUTION 13

Flex your way to success

In order to establish trust and successful communication with your prospect, you must consider his personality type. Matching his speed and style will make it easier for him to work with you. In the following exercise you reflect on the four basic personality types and consider what you can do to adapt to a communication/work style with which the prospect is comfortable

1. On a blank piece of paper, draw four separate quadrants, and write the four personality types in each box: Authoritative, Analytical, Influencer, Relational.

2. Below the word in each separate quadrant, nominate the primary characteristics that define each personality type.

3. Now, for each personality type, nominate the types of behaviors a person of that type would appreciate or expect to see present during a business meeting.

4. Next consider your personality type, and the speed, style, and behaviors you are comfortable with.

5. Thinking about your natural personality in relation to a specific prospect, nominate in each quadrant the manner in which you would have to flex to the other personality style in order to achieve the appropriate comfort level for a particular prospect. For example, you may have to present more information that you would usually do, or you may have to hone down your speaking style until it is concise and to the point.

6. When preparing to meet with your prospect, use the matrix to remind yourself how you need to flex for the personality type you are meeting.

ACTIVE LISTENING

The greatest compliment you can pay your customer is to listen to him. Not all salespeople are naturally good listeners, and indeed some believe their main purpose is to educate the prospect about their company or product. While it is important to do so at various times throughout the sales process, your main priority needs to be to find out what is important to your prospect, not what you think is important to him. Set yourself to understand him as fully as possible, focusing carefully on the responses your questions evoke.

Active listening is not the same as hearing, which is just processing sounds. When you are attentive to the true meaning of words, and the unspoken message behind them, you are engaging in active listening. In addition to hearing the facts directly from the customer's mouth, while actively listening, you are monitoring body language, emotion, and tone. Active listening means not only listening, but also understanding the other person, and in turn conveying that you have understood.

An added benefit to active listening is not only that you learn about your prospect's needs, but also that you may pick up all kinds of information about your competitors. Prospects tell you what they like and dislike about your competitors, as well as what they know about the potential future plans of other vendors. All extremely valuable information for you. This is certainly not the time to be thinking about what you are going to say next, or to let your mind wander or race.

Too many sales are lost simply because many salespeople have a tendency to talk instead of listen. How can you change that? You can start right now by making it a personal development goal. Not only will you see clear results in your professional life, you are bound to see added enhancements in your personal life as well. The following key points are vital to your listening success.

Prepare in advance. You can free your mind for active listening by preparing some of your questions and comments in advance. **Be ready to listen.** Focus on the customer, have paper and pen in hand, and take notes. If you are on the phone, let the customer know that you value his thoughts and that you are writing them down.

Make a goal. Focus all your concentration on understanding the buyer's needs, rather than thinking about what you are going to say next. Remember you are there to learn about his needs, goals, likes, and dislikes better than anyone else who has been through his door.

Limit your own talking. You cannot talk and listen at the same time. Hear the buyer out completely on each subject, and do not ever interrupt. Be careful not to complete the prospect's sentences for him. Evaluate the meaning of the prospect's words only when he has completed his thought.

Show you are listening. Be silent and attentive for face-to-face contacts, using your body language, posture, head nods, and steady eye-contact. For phone conversations, use attentive words: "Yes," "I see," "O.K." This reassures the customer that you are listening.

Do not interrupt. A pause, even a long pause does not mean he has finished saying everything he needs to say. Resist the temptation to fill silences with words. **Let him think.**

Filter out external distractions. Avoid looking around the office or at other people. Do not look at your watch. Just be with the customer.

Put yourself in the customer's shoes. His problems and needs are important, and you will understand and retain them better if you keep his point of view in mind.

Listen for ideas, not just words. Be sure you get the whole picture, not just isolated fragments.

React to the ideas, not the person. Do not become agitated at things the customer may be saying, or his manner in saying them. **Listen for content.** Avoid labeling, using stereotypes, or making negative judgments about the buyer.

Do not argue mentally. Keep an open mind while the customer is talking, even though you may disagree with his viewpoint. Otherwise you are likely to tune out.

Do not jump to conclusions. Avoid making assumptions about what the customer is thinking. **Let him tell you.**

Watch the non-verbals and listen to the overtones. You can learn a great deal about the customer from the way he says things and the manner in which he reacts to you. Monitor his voice, speech rate, volume, and what he chooses to emphasize.

Restate. Check your understanding. Do not just repeat what the prospect has said; rephrase the message in your own words. Use partial restatement. Do not restate the entire idea,

just the main points. The beauty of restatement is that it allows for course correction. If you are on target, it invites the buyer to agree with you. If you are off track, it allows for clarification, before you take action on the wrong idea.

Keep your prospect active. When he seems to be finishing up, attempt to re-engage him. Show your interest by asking a question. Use open questions to keep him talking.

Practice listening. As listening is so fundamental to your success, get into the habit immediately.

Remember that all new information you receive increases your knowledge, and that knowledge is power. Keep in mind all of the benefits of listening: You enhance the self-esteem of others by giving them space to have their views heard; you come across as genuine and intelligent; and you have a greater probability of not saying the wrong thing at the wrong time.

chapter 3

KEY SELLING SKILLS

The first stage of the Consultative Partnership Selling approach has been concerned with starting to build a relationship with a prospective client. The next step is to present the right product/service to that client and to show him that he is buying more than a physical object or a set of processes – what he is actually buying is a solution to his problems.

This chapter looks at the differences between a product's features and the benefits it represents to the client, and it shows how best to present and explain those benefits. It also looks at how to build the value of the product/service in the eyes of the client until the value exceeds the cost. Later, there is advice on how to respond to objections.

In today's ever more complex business world, salespeople who work business-to-business often find themselves confronted with panels of inquisitors. A major part of this chapter looks at the vital skill of presenting. It shows not only how to plan, practise, and put across an effective presentation, but also how to understand and balance the needs of a number of decision-makers at the same time.

UNDERSTANDING FEATURES AND BENEFITS

If a customer is willing to meet with you, he probably has a general notion of what it is you are selling. Indeed, early in the conversation you will have outlined some general benefits of the product/service in your Immediate Benefits Statement. However, it is only after you have learned about the client's needs that you can make him fully aware of all the ways your product/service could benefit him.

The term "feature" refers to a particular characteristic of a product, and the term "benefit" describes what is to be gained from that characteristic. Customers buy benefits, so it is important not to get carried away, discussing only features.

That is telling, not selling. It is the salesperson's job to translate features into customer advantage: How does the product make the prospect's business, life or job easier? How can it save time or money, alleviate pain, or reduce stress? What problems does it solve?

There is no need to inundate the client with detailed information about every characteristic of your offering. Only discuss features and benefits once you have learned about his needs, and limit your discussion to what is important to him.

There are two primary types of benefits: emotional and logical. Emotional benefits include happiness, serenity, security, balance, image, prestige, and popularity. Logical benefits include, for example, saving time and money, gaining technical advantage, streamlining processes, and improving safety.

Think for a moment how this applies to you when you are making a buying decision, perhaps a new telephone. You are looking at two models and Model A is twice the price of Model B. Both do what you expect a telephone to do. However, Model A has a three-year warranty (benefit: peace of mind), the manufacturer offers 24-hour customer service (benefit: convenience), the phone has redial (benefit: time saved) and is offered in a wide variety of colors (benefit: choice). If you attach importance to these "extras," you will likely buy the more expensive item despite the price difference.

Describe the features of your product/service that provide the benefits that you know the customer values and you are well on your way to helping him make important improvements in some part of his life or business.

BUILDING VALUE

The clearest way to distinguish yourself from your competitors is through your ability to add value to your prospect's business. The equation is simple: The value, or worth, of the product must be greater than the price. Establish the value by focusing on all the benefits your client finds advantageous.

So what are the essential ways you can establish, build, and maintain value? A popular starting point is to describe all the ways your product can reduce costs and increase revenues. There is typically a cost associated with purchasing any product/service, and this is not only the price tag, but also may include costs such as installation and staff training. Decision-makers are normally focused on how soon they can recover the initial investment in your product/service, as well as how the product can increase revenues. For example, if your product costs $25,000 but your client can increase his sales volume by $250,000 per year, the return on investment (ROI) timeframe is less than one month. Be prepared to discuss costs and returns.

While financial arguments can be very persuasive, it is important to fall out of the habit of focusing only on price, and instead emphasize all the other ways you can help your client build his business.

Take this example. Whenever a company purchases products and services that enhance its ability to serve customers, it may as a consequence dramatically increase customer retention, an important value-added.

With happy customers come happier employees. If employees are content, they are less likely to move on, and a lower employee turnover is another value-added.

The list of possible ways your product/service can add value is endless. Show your client how you can save him time, help him increase efficiencies, expedite delivery time frames, customize a service, add warranties, or minimize risks. Many selling organizations will also train their clients' employees on new systems and processes; another value-added.

Relationships are a big value builder that salespeople often forget to mention. Your ability as a salesperson to be responsive, reliable, knowledgeable, and helpful can be vitally important to clients. Knowing that you will deal with possible issues in a timely manner, the client is free to focus on other meaningful areas of the business.

All successful salespeople see the products/services they are selling in terms of the value that they can add to their customer's business. The better your ability to sell value of all kinds, the easier time you will have handling objections.

VALUE-ADDED

During my selling career I was in a position to suggest to my clients that they take on a toll-free number. However, many were nervous of the associated costs – they envisioned increased traffic that they could not control. In reality, though, when a company added the new lines and accompanied the launch with a direct-mail campaign informing their customers of the new numbers, there would invariably be two very positive and lucrative by-products. Predictably, there was an overall increase in customer satisfaction, but there was also a rapid and steady increase in sales volume. Clearly value-added!

PRESENTING SOLUTIONS

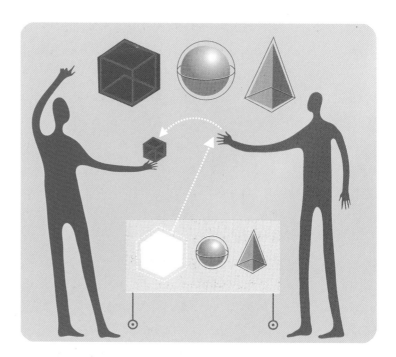

By using active listening and questioning skills during the fact-finding stage, you will have acquired a list of needs voiced by the customer. Now it is time to show the customer how your product/service can meet his needs. During the fact-finding stage, a good questioner will have encouraged the customer to think carefully about his own day-to-day circumstances, and to assess any problems that may have been brought to light. Presenting solutions to such problems and showing clearly how the solutions are specifically applied to the customer's circumstances follows on naturally from this.

Speak to the customer's needs and concerns: "When we last met you mentioned you have a problem with high staff turnover. Our service may be able to solve that for you by ....." Repeat his words back to him or paraphrase the concerns he expressed. Use examples from the experience of other (anonymous) clients: "They implemented the product and found it increased customer satisfaction almost overnight. They were able to reduce their complaints team by 40 percent in six months." Concrete statements relating to return on investment are important: Reducing a team by 40 percent represents a significant cost saving. Be on the lookout for such anecdotes when getting feedback from existing clients. Hard figures (percentage increases in revenue, decreases in costs, etc.) are very impressive.

Remember that the customer has a mental checklist, and is comparing your solutions to his own questions; which may include: "Is this a good value?" "How can this simplify my life?" "Who else has tried this?" and "Who will look after me if I decide to move forward with this?" How do you know what your customer is thinking? Through experience with others, through putting yourself in your customer's shoes, and through careful, active listening in the fact-finding phase.

REDIRECTING WANTS

Many salespeople have found themselves in the seemingly ideal situation in which a client calls up asking for a particular product from the range. However, beware. It is never wise simply to take the order. Instead, work through the fact-finding stage with the client as if this were any other transaction. In many cases accurate and careful questioning will show you that the client actually requires something other than the product he originally selected. It is your job to guide him to the optimal solution. In so doing you are more likely to create a bond of trust with him, leading, hopefully, to a mutually beneficial, long-lasting business partnership.

PRESENTATION SKILLS

Presentations are key opportunities for salespeople to communicate the potential value of their product/service as well as new skills and techniques. You may be a very knowledgeable and resourceful person, committed to forming long-term mutually beneficial relationships, but if you lack the ability to get your point across, no one is going to understand either the potential of your product/service to meet their needs or the benefits to be gained from taking you and your company on as a partner.

Effective presentations are attention-getting, meaningful, memorable, and activating. In other words, what you intend to say to your audience must capture their attention, speak to a specific need they have, make an impression, and move them to action.

Planning the content

As you begin thinking about your presentation, the first issue to be resolved is content. Even before you decide what it is you want to say, you must first consider your audience. Your goal must be to deliver a presentation that will meet the expertise level, needs, and expectations of your listeners, and the more advance knowledge you have about them, the greater your chances of success. The first step in audience analysis is to determine who will be attending, their positions in the organization, and their role in the decision-making process. You then need to consider what their attitudes might be toward your product/service, and be sure to look at this in relation to their position within the company, which

WORK SOLUTION 14

Organizing the content of your presentation

It is crucial that your presentation carries your audience from your starting point, through the different parts of the argument, to the conclusion. This five-step format will assist you in delivering an impacting presentation.

1. Create an opener. Focus your listeners' attention right from the outset using quotations, rhetorical questions, anecdotes, real-world situations. Avoid apologies; long, complex or slow-moving statements; obvious observations; trite questions; or stories unrelated to your topic.

2. State the three main points or topics. Provide listeners with an overview of your presentation so they understand its direction. Draw listeners in by stating the points in terms of their company's needs or current issues.

3. Develop transitions, joining the end of one point to the beginning of the next, providing a natural flow between points.

4. Present the solution. Now is the time to talk about what your company's products and services can do to address the problems and issues the client is experiencing. It is also the perfect time to allow audience members to "touch and feel" your products and services by demonstrating how they work.

5. The conclusion needs to move your audience to action by reminding them how switching to your service will "make life more palatable." Summarize your main points using vivid imagery, which leaves your group members with a compelling and positive image of you, your organization, and your products and services.

determines their point of reference. Endeavor to maximize the usefulness of your presentation for your attendees by making it completely relevant to their interests.

Keep in mind also what the objective of the meeting is. Is it a presentation designed for basic introduction, or does it come at a more advanced stage in the process? You will also have your own objective, and this will affect the content you choose to deliver. Being clear on these points will make planning the main message less difficult.

Once you understand who your meeting participants will be, and your primary goal, you are ready to begin thinking about what you want to say. You can help determine the content by asking yourself, "What are the benefits to the

listeners of what I have to say?" and, "What action would I like my prospect to take as a result of the meeting/presentation?" Your answers should be very specific and clear, and should be the primary thought you would like your listeners to walk away with and reflect upon. This single most important thought is referred to as your "point of view." When your listeners are asked what you said, this is the sentence they should repeat. Once you have determined your point of view, ask yourself the following four questions to better ensure its effectiveness: "Will your point of view make sense to your listeners?" "Do you believe it?" "What is the benefit to the audience of what you have to say?" "Is it clear and concise?"

The following points may also help to guide you as you put together the content for your presentation.

• **Listeners bring their life experience to the meeting room.** Your prospects are knowledgeable about many topics and have learned concepts and skills throughout their lives. You can use this to the benefit of all members of your audience by allowing individuals to share their knowledge with others as it relates to your product or service line. If possible discover the existing knowledge level of your attendees with respect to your product line, and speak to that level. Respect their time and do not over-stress things your participants already know, or appear to be grasping quickly.

• **Your listeners will be connecting what they are hearing to what they already know.** With a lifetime of experiences, we tend to categorize what we know. As we learn new things, we fit them into these categories. Help your attendees to do this by referring them often to situations or concepts that are familiar to them while you are explaining new things.

• **Adults have ingrained habits.** Your participants already have their own way of doing things, and your proposal may represent totally new methods. Be flexible, respectful of your listeners' skills, and open to questions and suggestions. Help your participants discover how adapting to new ways of doing things will benefit them.

Visual Aids

In public speaking we deliver our message through three channels of communication: visual 55 percent, vocal 38 percent, and verbal 7 percent. As members of an audience, we tend to be stimulated more by visual input than by aural input. Because of this visual aids can be used to great effect, but conversely they can also divert attention from what we are saying. Using slides outlining your argument can help you be concise when speaking, but the wording should be short and succinct so that your listeners can read them quickly and then turn their attention back to what you are saying.

Visuals such as diagrams and graphs (keep them simple and clear) help the audience to gain a deeper understanding of your argument. They enable you to elaborate on examples and make figures and trends more tangible. Make sure you can explain each graphic simply, and when you have finished move on to the next slide, so that your audience's attention does not linger with the graphic. Finally, don't be afraid of

WORK SOLUTION 15

Involve your audience

Involving your audience is a surefire way to make sure they feel like an interested, integral part of your presentation. The next time you are planning a talk before an audience, consult the following checklist, which will help you insure that you are dynamic and effective.

1. Encourage audience attention, interaction, and participation by asking a question. Asking for a show of hands or directing your listeners to think back to a specific situation are effective means of keeping them tuned in.

2. Reference facts and figures that bolster your message. The use of simple statistical data that is easily remembered can highlight the importance of your message and give it added credibility.

3. Quote a well-known or respected authority or literary figure. Give your presentation added meaning and perspective by finding a way to tie it in to what a famous philosopher or business person had to say on the subject matter.

4. Use appropriate drama, movement, or humor to bring a sense of urgency and importance to your message.

5. Visuals, product samples, and product demonstrations are particularly good methods of achieving and maintaining audience interest.

6. Think of your presentation as storytelling. This will make it less intimidating for you, and will help you to remember that it needs to be interesting for your audience as well as informative.

displaying a blank screen, or a screen with your company logo, if you have no information to put across visually.

OVERCOMING PRESENTATION ANXIETY

Presenting to large groups is, for almost everyone, a major source of trepidation. Indeed, some even break out in a cold sweat just thinking about having to make a speech. Of course, a certain amount of anxiety is good: It increases your epinephrine (adrenalin) level and ensures you perform well. But too much anxiety can be debilitating.

By far the most effective remedy for presentation anxiety is preparation. Complete your presentation a week in advance if you can, and then practice running through every part of it, in order, every day, working with any audio-visuals you have chosen. Memorizing your presentation word-for-word is not recommended. Anxiety can cause you to blank out, and a memorized speech can appear unnatural and insincere. Instead use your computer presentation or cue cards for the main points and practice elaborating on them, looking for different and ever more effective ways of getting each point across. Find out from the organizer how much time you have been allotted and make sure your presentation falls comfortably within that timeframe without having to rush.

Check your equipment on the day of the presentation, in time to re-organize or replace items if need be. Before the meeting get access to the venue and ensure that the room is arranged and set up as you need it to be. Familiarity with your surroundings and being certain the equipment is working should go a long way toward calming a fluttering stomach.

As the meeting begins make sure that you have time to walk around the room introducing yourself to the participants. Fear of the unknown is one of our biggest fears as humans, and creating a warm and friendly environment in this way will help reduce your anxiety.

Your objective in making your presentation is to connect with your audience so that each individual member will understand, remember, and assimilate your message. What you project should fit the context, support your message, and awaken and involve your listeners. When you present in a style that relates to your listeners, energizes, enthuses, and moves them to action, you have successfully created a compelling presentation.

SELLING TO MULTIPLE DECISION-MAKERS

The larger the company you are dealing with in the sales process, and the greater the potential revenue volume of the account, the more likely it is that you will be communicating with more than just one decision-maker. This is referred to as a "complex sale," in which it is necessary to coordinate your response to several layers of needs, different areas of individual responsibility, and perhaps several stages of approval. Such situations require strong analytical skills.

The first step in this type of selling environment is to meet all the team members and determine what their decision-making process will be.

It is important and useful early on to verify who is your main interface in the group. This person will be your main point of contact, and working through him will streamline the process. This person is likely to be responsible for internal communication within the group, as well as setting up meetings and taking care of practical issues.

Meeting the team should be your next priority. At your first presentation, or introductory meeting, make sure you take the time to meet all of the individuals involved. Use your questioning and rapport-building skills to learn a little about each member of the team. Once you have introduced yourself and set the tone for the meeting, say something to the effect of, "Now I'd like to go around the room and learn a little about each one of you. We can start with a personal introduction, and then if you'd please tell me your own objective for today's session, as well as your role in the buying process." By the end of the introductions you will already

be starting to understand who is who, and what each person's concerns are. You should also have a good idea of how the decision-making process will be handled. Be prepared, however, for decision-making processes to change down the line.

Although several people may have been asked to evaluate your products/services, they may not all be decision-makers. Some or all of them may be "coaches," nominated to gather information about a specific product/service, and then report back on their findings. It is likely that such individuals will be making internal presentations on your products/services, so it is important to supply them with all the data and support materials they need.

In some businesses the policy may be to bring together staff from different departments in order to facilitate a complex decision. The interests of each individual will, in this case, naturally reflect the concerns and functions of the

department they represent. You may find yourself dealing with several decision-makers, such as a financial buyer, a technical buyer, a marketing/sales buyer, and other buyers representing key departments. The person representing finance is likely to be looking to improve the profits of the organization, either by directly increasing sales or by reducing costs. He may also be concerned with the cost of the product/service and its implementation. The person representing marketing may be far less concerned with financial impact, and far more focused on image and branding issues and how they can be used to enhance sales. The technical buyer will want to ensure that the product is actually necessary, meets the company's technical requirements, and will not cause any technical problems. He may also be thinking about training and installation issues.

When working with a group, you will not only be dealing with different professional and organizational needs and concerns, but also with the whole gamut of personality types. You will find dominant as well as passive personalities. You will have the "know-it-all" as well as the "I couldn't care less about this" types. And, of course, each team member has a different relationship with every other member – look out for internal politics.

Your true skill as a salesperson will come into play when you take each of the individual considerations into account, address them accordingly, and present your product in such a way that you satisfy all of their requirements. Listen carefully to each individual in turn, cover each issue of concern and

always relate the benefit in terms of the value it would bring and the specific ways it meets the needs expressed. Make sure you involve each of the participants. Feed back each person's concern to the group and address it specifically: "Mr. Jones, you mentioned your concerns about (current levels of materials wastage; high employee turnover; high transport costs; etc.). Let's take a look at how our (the product) could work with you to solve that issue." Once you have presented your service in terms of a specific participant's need, ask: "How does that sound to you?" And wait for a response. Then ask: "Do you have any other points thus far you'd like me to expand upon, or any concerns?" Make sure you address each of the individual's concerns as they arise, and then move on to the next participant. Move from person to person without hurrying, addressing each individual perspective until you've satisfied all points.

Be careful not to take sides or to minimize anyone's concern. Equally, avoid overtly focusing on one indivdual – such as the team leader – and neglecting others. Remember to be as equal in your treatment of all team members as you possibly can, even though some may appear less influential than others and one or two may emerge as your favorites.

The way to maximize success when selling to multiple decision-makers is to do so on a person-by-person basis. When you gain the approval of each individual, you will earn the consent of the whole group.

RESOLVING CONCERNS

Resolving concerns can be one of the most stressful parts of the selling process. Some salespeople believe that customers raise concerns only as they become more interested in a competing product. This makes them nervous because they think the sale may be slipping away. Some view the raising of objections as confrontational, and so try to avoid situations where objections might be raised or actively discussed. And some simply don't know how to answer or address their customer's concerns effectively, and thus become intimidated.

But the raising of objections doesn't mean "No." Objections occur throughout the sales process and are necessary and vital steps in moving forward, and thus they are actually a very desirable part of interacting with your customer, of finding out what he really thinks. It is more about keeping the

dialogue open, similar to making a move in a chess game, inviting a move from you. This is good news for you: Objections prolong the dialogue and allow the rapport between you and the customer to grow. Objections are a signal that he is interested in what you are saying, and are frequently a way of having his questions answered.

Top sales performers realize that customers raise objections and concerns for a variety of reasons. Basically, there are three main reasons why a customer voices objections: Interest in a competitive product; a need for additional information; or a need to reinforce the correctness of their decision.

The most common objection in the selling profession, regardless of the product or service, is price. All salespeople must make themselves familiar with the price objection. A customer typically says, "It costs too much" when they are not convinced of the value of your product/service; that the benefits exceed the cost. The value is to be found in the sum benefits or the worth of your product. As discussed earlier you establish the value of your product by educating through the use of features and benefits. The value (worth) of your product must be greater than the price.

Other common objections and how to respond to them:

"We've heard some negative reports about your company and its product."

Interpret this as a request for you to show proof of improvements.

"I'm not sure you're offering what I need."

The unstated objection here may be that your customer is not sure you can meet his needs, or does not perceive your product/service as any better than the one he is currently using. The response here would be to offer specifically targeted solutions to his issues, and if he does not perceive your product/service as better than the one he has, provide more distinctions and differentiations.

"I need to think about it."

What may actually be going on in the mind of the prospect when he says this is fear of making the wrong decision. Take what actions you can to make your customer feel more comfortable: For example, ask if he would like to speak to other happy and satisfied customers, visit your facilities, gain a clearer understanding of your company's commitment to post-sale service.

"I disagree with what you're saying."

Hearing this you need to start by clarifying your prospect's reasons for disagreement by asking what he has heard or knows to be different from the information you have provided, and then carefully answer each point.

Remember, there are times when objections may be temporarily insurmountable – it is not realistic to expect a sale every time. As long as you remain honest and professional, you have done the most you can do, and you want to be remembered for it. I once worked for a long-distance phone company that had recently gone through a merger and took more than a year to integrate its billing system. As a result bills were frequently issued three months in arrears and sometimes with incorrect data. I found myself selling to a large client for whom timely billing was crucial because the company was re-selling its phone service to other tenants. I had to tell the client that at this time our service would not be appropriate for his company. I had to walk away from the sale – my company simply could not have met this all-important need at that time. However, I had established excellent rapport with the client, and he called me back eight months later, when he moved to another company, and wanted to revisit our service.

Objections are only temporary obstacles. They show that your prospect is thinking about moving forward with you, but needs a little more information and reassurance. Think of objections as buying signals, and remember the only time you need to worry is when your prospect does not voice them.

SIX RULES FOR RESOLVING CONCERNS

1: Listen
Hear the customer out. Once the customer has completed his thought, ask questions only that clarify his concerns and the reason he is raising them.

2: Verify your understanding
Make sure you have uncovered and understood all of the objections the client has at the time. Do not be afraid to look for more, because with each objection you overcome, you are one step closer to an agreement.

3: Ask questions
Never argue with a customer in response to an objection. Instead, further involve him by asking probing questions that get him to elaborate on his reasons and expectations. Thank him.

4: Reframe
This tool is used when the customer is focusing on one small issue. Relate the objection that the customer has voiced into the overall "big picture." Refer back to what the initial customer need was, and all of the ways the solution fulfills that need. Confirm agreement: "Does that make sense?" or "Would you agree?"

5: Summarize
Put into your own words all the key objections the customer has raised and your responses to those concerns. Give the customer an opportunity to agree or disagree, by asking, "Did I understand you correctly?" If the answer is negative, correct your course.

6: Confirm that you have resolved all the customer's concerns
The only way to know for sure if you have satisfied your prospect is to ask. If you have done so, nice job! If not, repeat the process until you clarify the customer's true position and are certain you understand it.

NEGOTIATING

The simple term "negotiating" conjures up a variety of images and expectations for most of us. Perhaps we think in terms of world politics, labor disputes, the process of purchasing a car or a house, or the on-going give and take between spouses and with children. Negotiation is a constant presence in our lives, and at some level we are conditioned to negotiate with those around us from our earliest years.

Negotiating is a process between two or more parties with the aim of achieving common ground. Negotiations have four potential outcomes, and ideally we should approach each negotiation opportunity with a view to creating a positive outcome for everyone. In the Consultative Partnership Selling approach, this end result should be your main consideration. The four possible outcomes are: win-lose, lose-win, lose-lose, win-win.

• **Win-lose.** In this situation the salesperson, for example, makes the sale at a hefty profit, and the buyer could have fared better elsewhere. The salesperson feels like a winner, the buyer feels like he lost out.

• **Lose-win.** In the lose-win situation, the seller, for example, sells his home for well under the market price. The seller feels like a loser, or perhaps he feels taken advantage of, and the buyer feels like a winner, as he just made an instant profit at the expense of the seller.

• **Lose-lose.** The lose-lose situation is a really undesirable scenario for all concerned; something we would call "bad business." In this situation neither the salesperson nor the customer is satisfied. An example of this would be where a

salesperson agrees to sell a product below cost, resulting in little or no profit for his company, and the customer determines that he really has no use for the product or service.

• **Win-win.** In the win-win situation, the prospect is happy to have become a customer, likes the product, and is content with the overall terms and conditions; and the salesperson is a winner because he has acquired a new customer for his company and has met the customer's needs.

As our goal is to create the most possible win-win situations in our negotiating opportunities, let us take a look at how best to go about laying the foundation for such an outcome. The first step is to enter the negotiation with an enthusiastic and friendly attitude, rather than an adversarial one.

Always begin your dialogue by reviewing the "positives," the points on which you are in agreement. Avoid an argumentative climate by being respectful of the other person's position. Maintain respect by refusing to argue, be dismissive of, or accusatory toward your colleague. Remember that you are there to resolve issues for him.

Typically, in any negotiation issue, there is one main "sticking point" accompanied by a sub-set of minor issues. To create the most positive outcome, make your points of discussion very specific, but avoid having the entire negotiation hinge on just one issue. This may easily lead to a win-lose outcome. A perfect example of this would be if your customer has a specific budget for a product, but the product is 20 percent more expensive than this figure. Instead of getting into a pricing battle, focus on other points to make the price more palatable to the customer. Introduce extended warranties, financing, training, or any of the host of other "extras" your company may be happy to supply.

To succeed in win-win negotiating, focus on the issue, and gain agreement step by step by stating the points on which you both agree. Be solution-oriented, and do not become emotional. Have a clear goal in mind, which includes mutually agreed upon shared interests, and think in terms of whatever you need to do to achieve the goal.

Creating an outcome that makes your customer feel satisfied, and at the same time allows you to fulfill your business requirements will be your smartest negotiating strategy.

WORK SOLUTION 16

Creating a WIN-WIN situation

As life becomes increasingly demanding and more complex, your ability to negotiate becomes more important. Successful negotiation requires open-mindedness, skill, practice, time, and patience. By practicing the following negotiation principles and skills, negotiating can become a tool for conflict resolution, part of your daily approach to managing relationships professionally, at home, and in your community.

1. Reflect on an issue or sticking point you wish to resolve. Begin by recognizing and defining the problem by writing a statement of what you want or need in the situation. Now do the same again, but this time from the perspective of what you think your counterpart wants or needs. Remember negotiation must clearly identify not only individual concerns, but also mutual concerns, perceptions, and interests.

2. Show respect. Be soft on the person, hard on the problem. Success rests in accepting the other person regardless of differences in perspective. Negotiation allows you to examine a problem from all sides, and to promote an understanding of the other person without necessarily agreeing to his viewpoint.

3. Brainstorm. This allows each party to make suggestions without fear of criticism, and allows you to seek a variety of solutions. Negotiation becomes a matter of choosing a solution to which no-one objects, and shared goals take precedence over personal goals.

4. Review. At this stage every suggestion has value and is accepted. Review to determine where suggestions might coincide or overlap with one another.

5. Collaborate. All negotiated work is completed by consensus.

WHEN TO CLOSE

Closing is the process of getting final agreement to your proposal. If you consistently have agreement as you move through each step of the sale, closing becomes the natural culmination of the sales process. People love to buy. As salespeople we don't need to force people to buy our product or service, we just have to allow them to participate in the sale and feel good about the choices they have made. Buyers want to buy, but before they do they want to feel like they are in competent hands: yours.

Closing is not a process reserved for the tail end of the sales call. It is really all about relationships. Closing means being in agreement and gaining commitment, and this is something you are doing every step of the way throughout

your customer interaction. If you demonstrate an ability to partner with and understand your customer by speaking in terms of his interests and concerns, it is likely that he is going to trust you with an effective solution to his needs. So, if you are doing everything properly, you should feel confident in asking for his business, without the use of any hard sell or manipulative tactics.

In the world of sales, timing is everything, and knowing how and when to ask your prospect about his readiness to partner with you and move forward in achieving his business goals, is nothing mysterious. The key is, as always, to be aware of the unconscious signals that your customer is giving you. Certain signals, such as certain questions, show you that the client is ready to buy, but sometimes we are so focused on our own thoughts that we talk right past our prospect's signs of interest. These signals usually occur suddenly, and are seen in a shift in the behavior of the buyer. Be on the lookout for two types of buying signals: verbal and behavioral.

The verbal signals may include the following:

• The prospect asks specific questions about what will happen after the order is signed: for example, he talks about discount structures or staff training.

• The prospect tells you that he has talked to other happy customers of yours and is impressed.

• He mentions that your product is exactly what he is looking for.

• He says that it is not necessarily the least expensive, but then again, anything worth having is not always the cheapest.

• The prospect acknowledges that the product is a real problem-solver for his particular company's circumstances.

Behavioral signs to be watchful of include:
• Leaning forward, nodding the head, open and expansive gestures, and smiling.
• Taking the salesperson around the office to meet other people in the company, or even perhaps introducing you to the person with whom you would interact post-sale.

When you get a clear buying signal, it is important that you use your questioning skills to verify it. Be careful not to make inaccurate assumptions. This is especially true with the physical buying signals because they are more open to interpretation than actual words, which are specific. For example, a prospect who picks up your product to have another look at it may be re-examining something he is not too keen about. Equally, someone who is looking over your paperwork might have some issues with it. Some clarification questions you may consider asking are: "How does this seem?" "What are your thoughts?" "Would you agree that this would meet your needs at this time?"

Never risk making your prospect feel manipulated or pressured. Look for a clear affirmative response to your verification questions. Be careful not to proceed if you just have silence. If the prospect is hesitant, try to identify the cause by asking, "Can I clarify anything for you?" or "I feel you may have a concern."

Correctly evaluating your prospect's buying signals helps you to verify that your proposal is on target, and if it is not, it allows you to make the proper course correction. You may need to engage with further concerns or objections, or it may be that your product/service simply is not right for this client at this time. Being sensitive to the client's signals demonstrates your professionalism and integrity and ensures that you do not miss out on the opportunity of continuing to work with him in the future.

Some salespeople find this moment in the sales process the hardest. It may simply be that they fear rejection. After all, they have invested a lot of effort in learning who the customer is, what his business and personal needs are, and endeavoring to fulfill them through the product/service. But by the time you come to the closing step of the sale, you should have had sufficient time in the process to achieve trust and rapport and to obtain an overall high level of understanding with your prospect. In a relaxed and friendly environment such as this, asking for commitment – closing – should simply be a natural progression.

A very natural and effective way to start the ball rolling in this direction – toward attaining commitment from your prospect – is to make sure first that you have covered all objections, and second that you have a buying signal and have verified that this signal is accurate. Then simply re-focus the dialogue. Summarize the four or five main points that you have between you decided are his company's main needs. Then simply ask.

chapter 4

STAYING MOTIVATED

Sales is one of those careers in which you are exposed to a lot more "Nos" than "Yeses." Much of your sales success hinges upon your ability to stay focused, resist the negative effects of rejection, pick yourself up, and pursue your goals. After a setback the easiest thing to do is to give up, do a little less and blame your company, the product, or other people, but in the long run this is counterproductive. Sales is a process of setting and achieving goals. Overcoming obstacles is just part of the challenge that goes with the profession.

This chapter looks at ways to stay motivated even when the going gets tough. It shows how to ensure that your whole life is adequately balanced and oriented to the values that you espouse, and looks at how your personal resources can sustain you through the difficult times. You will learn how to bolster your resilience in the face of rejection, and how to bring balance and harmony into your fast-paced life.

In addition this chapter outlines some practical techniques for staying motivated, including tips for handling rejection, and advice for keeping your selling skills finely honed.

MAINTAINING BALANCE AND HARMONY

It is almost a prerequisite for the sales profession that you are prepared to put in a lot of time and energy in order to succeed. However, while there is nothing wrong with putting your career first, there is a danger in making it your whole life. Those who live to work often find themselves subject to the law of diminishing returns: the harder they work, the less productive they are, not only at work, but in other areas of their lives as well, and it may also affect their health.

I have a cousin in Europe, a veterinary professor. At the end of his university day, Antun worked at a veterinary clinic. However, the 14-hour days took their toll on his health and his family missed his attention. Looking at his priorities Antun finally took the decision to scale back his work at the clinic. Although the extra money was sorely missed, he soon noticed his blood pressure normalizing. His muscular tension disappeared, his family benefited from his greater presence, and he was able to pursue non-professional interests.

In order to create a balance between your professional and your personal life, you need to expand your range of vision. Make a "life audit" as described in Work Solution 17, opposite. Compare the notes you made about what you value with the reality of your daily life. If there is a mismatch, start thinking about what changes to make in order to find more time for the things that make you whole.

WORK SOLUTION 17

Making a life audit

We all have areas of our lives we would like to change or re-direct. Perhaps you lack adequate time for family and friends, or have unexplored hobbies you would like to pursue but never seem to get around to. Many of us also spend time on activities that are without value. They soak up our time and drain our energy. Understanding how our priorities match our daily activities is the first step in restoring balance to our lives.

1. With paper and pen in hand, consider all the dimensions in your life in which you place value. Enjoy this first step. Write down your ideals, your craziest ideas, and your dreams. When you are done, prioritize the items.

2. Next, keep track for two weeks how you spend your time. Include such items as: Your main work activities, commuting, cooking, eating, housekeeping, shopping, leisure activities, fitness routines, spiritual pursuits, family time, etc.

3. At the end of the two-week period, count up the number of hours you spend on each activity and compare this with the list of values and priorities you made at the outset. Make a note of any discrepancies you find – areas where you are perhaps spending too much time on activities you loathe and too little time on activities that conform to your ideals.

4. Now look again at the list of activities you made and determine which are draining your energy reserves. Keep in mind that your reserves can be drained just as easily by guilt over things you are not doing as by things you are doing. Procrastination is a big energy drain, sucking up energy and producing nothing.

5. Now you should have a clearer idea of how your daily life conforms with your ideals, and where in particular certain activities are depleting your reserves of energy. Having made your "life audit" you are ready to chart your new agenda, by determining which activities to prioritize and which to minimize or eliminate from your life altogether.

DEFINING PERSONAL GOALS

Imagine setting out on a journey. You walk along the road without a destination in mind and with no map or compass. For now you simply enjoy the view and keep walking. Eventually, though, it starts to rain. You get hungry, cold, and tired. Sitting down by the side of the road, you begin to ask yourself, "Where am I going anyway, and why?" In the same way, when the going gets tough in our professional lives, we often ask ourselves similar questions: "Why am I doing this? What's the point?" At these times it would be helpful to know where we are going and how we think we can get there, and not only in our work, but in all aspects of our lives.

Goal-setting allows you access to your objectives by increasing your level of effectiveness and efficiency; and we all know that when we have clear direction we can also keep our motivation alive. Knowing that our destination is only another 20 minutes along the road, we keep walking, despite the rain.

In selling your professional goals are likely to be driven by your quota, set by the company. In your personal life, it is up to you to define your own goals. Start by making an audit of your personal values and comparing them to your everyday life as described Work Solution 17 (see page 115). What comes out of this should be a series of intentions. Now turn the intentions into goals that are tangible and specific. For example, if you have decided you need to allocate more family time, do not just nominate that as your goal, but rather turn it into an "action item" by deciding which days and hours of the week you intend to spend with your family. If your goal is a concrete achievement (perhaps you wish to study for a professional exam, or save enough money to travel abroad), set a time limit, and work out what you have to do each day, week, or month to achieve your goal within the set time. It is important to not only set the goal, but also to have a realistic idea of what it is going to take to get there.

Make it a point to share your new goals with close family and friends so they can be supportive of your efforts, and assist you in staying on track. When you are accountable not only to yourself, but also to your "inner-circle," you will find that you will strive more actively to fulfill your goals. Remember also that the STAR principle (see page 40) can be just as useful in defining personal goals as it is in defining professional goals.

By defining and planning your personal goals, focusing on them, and committing to their evolution, you will be well on your way to achieving the success you deserve.

DEVELOPING A PERSONAL MISSION STATEMENT

Whenever I teach a seminar to new hires, I often start by taking a look at their company's mission statement. The purpose behind a mission statement is to outline what the company values. The mission statement is intended as a statement of abstract belief on which the actions of all of its employees are based. It reflects a joint company philosophy, attitude, and expectations.

Once, while conducting a training program for a soft-drink manufacturer, we reviewed the corporate mission statement, which was similar in tone to: "We are a dynamic, hard-working, flexible, customer-oriented organization, constantly adapting to the changing needs of our market … etc." One student commented, "I really don't like change, I prefer consistency, and quite frankly customers are not my cup of tea!"

I pointed out to the student that it was very important that he recognized that fact immediately, because perhaps he was not employed by an organization whose goals and values were very similar to his. Whenever this is the case, there will be dissonance between you and the organization. Demotivation and disillusionment typically creep in.

To prevent internal strife of this sort, it is useful to formulate your own mission statement, which outlines your sense of purpose and direction, so that more

often than not, you find yourself where you want to be, doing the things you want to be doing with people of like mind.

In order to develop a meaningful mission statement, you will need to include four key points. The first thing to consider are your personal values. Think about qualities and abstract ideas, such items as: integrity, creativity, education, responsibility, partnerships, loyalty, achievement, professional growth, serving others, etc. Next, think about how you can integrate your values so that they are part of your daily life. Then consider how your mission statement affects your colleagues and family members. And finally list all the benefits you can reap from living in a fulfilling manner, binding your values to your professional and personal goals.

Perhaps the greatest success in life is living in accordance with your own values. Developing a personal mission statement will assist you on that path.

A MAN WITH A MISSION

I have a cousin who was a very successful partner in a prestigious law firm, which employed 70 attorneys. Steve was putting in 12-hour days for many years, and although he was successful and had a very happy home life, he did not feel fulfilled and he was experiencing a high level of internal conflict. It took him quite a lot of time spent in self-reflection to determine that the people he was spending most of his life with (his colleagues and partners) had very different values from his own, and he finally realized that he would prefer to be among people who shared his vision and perspective on life. His solution was to take a look at his personal mission statement, to re-write it, to make his own script. In so doing he gathered the courage to resign and form his own law firm, hiring people he knew to be of like mind. Once Steve made the proper corrections in life, and was living in accordance with his own beliefs and values, his anxieties disappeared.

TIME-MANAGEMENT

In all parts of our lives, time is a finite and therefore vastly important commodity. How we organize and use our time can mean the difference between professional success and failure or between attaining our personal goals and missing out. Firm time-management can help improve our performance at work and can also give us a way to balance the demands of our career with our need for variety and depth in our personal lives. Both of these have a direct influence on our levels of motivation at work.

Starting to manage your time requires an initial audit, so that you are aware of the current situation. As before (see page 115), keep a diary for two weeks or so, but this time include in more detail all the different activities you undertake from hour to hour. Include not only your work activities, but also the things you do in your personal life, and do not forget "downtime" activities, such as listening to the news, showering, etc. Take note in particular of occasions when you felt time was wasted: for example, time spent fruitlessly searching for something or retracing your steps because you forgot to do or say something.

After you have completed your audit, analyze it as before, this time giving each activity a score depending on how important it is in meeting your professional and personal goals. Ask yourself, "How long do the various activities take?" "Is this the best use of my time?" "How many of my tasks could be completed simultaneously (such as catching up with the business press over lunch)?"

The next step is to replan your time. Don't be rigid; be

realistic. Whenever possible eliminate procrastination. As the saying goes procrastination is the thief of time. If you know that there are tasks you consistently put off, force yourself to tackle them right away.

Commit to electronic communication and paperwork only once daily. So much time is wasted reading e-mails throughout the day, and then later going back to respond to them. Switch off the e-mail alert on your PC so that it does not disturb your concentration while you are engaged in other tasks. Get closer to your goal of being a successful sales-person by not using precious selling hours for planning and paperwork activities.

So how do you begin to organize and manage your time? We cannot go completely against our natural tendencies. We all have a time of day when we are at our best, when our creativity and our energy levels are at their peak. This is the time

we will be most productive. Schedule the activities you ranked as top priority for this time. Undertake simple, routine tasks that require less creativity or emotional energy for the time when you know you have less.

Plan your time by scheduling a month, a week, and 24 hours in advance. Make a daily "To Do List," and rank each task in an order that reflects your priorities. Avoid time-wastage by, for example, confirming your appointments the day before. There is nothing worse than driving out to a meeting that has been canceled.

So that your daily activities can be viewed with enthusiasm as often as possible, add variety to your schedule. Whenever we get bored, or we are faced with a stream of tasks of the variety we least enjoy, we tend to lose focus and motivation. The best way to minimize the chances of this happening is to make your days interesting and varied.

When I was managing my time as a salesperson, I typically allocated Mondays and Fridays as office days. On these days we had morning staff meetings, and I used the afternoons for cold-calling and appointment-getting. On Tuesdays, Wednesdays, and Thursdays I was in my territory meeting with my clients. The beauty of organizing your schedule in such a way is that your clients and co-workers get to know your routine and understand your availability. This is a great help in minimizing distractions and interruptions.

Learn to discourage interruptions by being politely assertive. If you have allocated the afternoon for cold-calling, place a sign on your door or cubicle letting others know not to interrupt you. Tell them you can better focus on their concern when you are not in the middle of another important task. But don't cut yourself off from your colleagues — let them know when you will have quality time for them.

I cannot stress enough the importance of not doing paperwork during time periods when you could be communicating with customers and prospects. Reserve these tasks for quiet hours, such as evenings or early mornings. You are likely to find that you will maximize your effectiveness with both your clients and your paperwork because you will be more focused.

Another great tool in maximizing your productivity is to clean up the clutter around you. It is far easier to concentrate when your work area is working for you, not against you. So much time is wasted searching for misplaced items, and the building frustration you feel during the search is always counterproductive.

Of course, these days there is a whole host of computerized options to help you organize your time, and your company may already have a preference. However, not all software options are suitable for everyone. We all have different ways of working, and some maintain that a handwritten calendar and notebook are best. If you have the option, take time to assess available software, and use the product that best enables you to manage your time most effectively.

HANDLING REJECTION

The selling profession by definition is subject to its fair share of ebb and flow. The highs are the part salespeople live for; the lows need to be carefully navigated. All salespeople, irrespective of how long they have been in sales, experience refusals and set-backs. The first step in coping with rejection, is to expect it as a normal by-product of your profession. Be realistic. Keep in mind that famous actors, singers, artists, writers, and the like are all subject to numerous rejections before they get their "big break." Their greatness is not measured by the amount of times they "strike out," but rather by their persistence, their ability to keep on keeping on.

Anticipate rejection and use it as a learning experience. Think of it as an opportunity to re-evaluate your skills, and

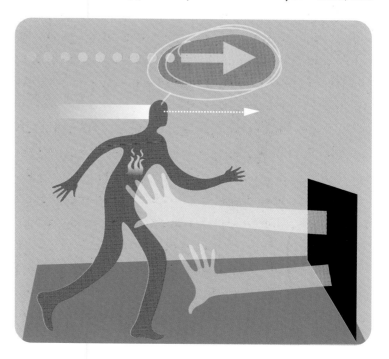

therefore grow as a professional. Whenever I would lose a sale, I made it a habit to ask the prospect what the specific factors were that lead to the loss of the sale. This was very useful information for me as a salesperson, because it allowed me to review my personal approach, as well as the product/prospect fit. Through this technique I learned many things: How to improve my qualifying, listening, and analytical skills, to name only a few.

Remember to separate yourself from your product. This is not to say that you should be detached or uncaring; simply understand that if a prospect finds fault with some feature or element of your product or service, they are not finding fault with you personally. Perhaps at this time your product does not suit their particular needs, or the business argument for staying with an existing supplier is stronger than changing to you. But by all means do what you can to stay in touch. Your product will undoubtedly be enhanced, and the customer may modify his requirements.

If a person is rude or terse with you, remember that just like you, they have their good days and their not so good days. I used to have a manager who reminded my team, "You never know whose dog died yesterday." We all try to juggle life's challenges the best we can, some days we are not as successful as others. Keep it in perspective and move on.

When you initiate thoughtful actions toward others, you are immediately gratified by a sense of personal satisfaction. A movement was initiated several years ago which encouraged people to "Practice random acts of kindness and senseless beauty." Simply put: Surprise total strangers with an act of kindness. If you have just lost an important sale, try this method for an instant pick-me-up. I experienced this not long ago when I was crossing a toll plaza. When I offered my $5 to the attendant, he informed me that the driver in front of me just paid my toll! This not only made my day, it also encouraged me immediately to think of what I could do for someone else. I enjoyed telling other people about my experience, and I quickly realized that the idea really works, spreading positive feeling from person to person.

Whatever your remedy for the blues that come from rejection, try not to resort to addictive or obsessive behavior. Alcohol and drugs, overeating or binge-shopping may take your mind off your temporary failure, but of course activities like these can only in the end be destructive. Be aware of your natural responses to rejection, and try to ensure that they are positive rather than negative.

Always remember that the selling profession is only one element of your life. It is not your totality, nor should you ever define yourself in terms of your profession. Jobs come and go, and professions change, but you as a whole person remain constant. Be careful not to fall into the increasingly common trap of basing your self-worth and identity on your job status or monthly sales ranking. Even the most successful salespeople wade through a sea of rejections. Taking rejection as a daily fact of your professional life and knowing what the effective antidotes are will help to keep rejections in perspective and give you the energy to persevere.

WORK SOLUTION 18

Maintaining a positive, motivated attitude

Your career as a sales professional is filled with many highs and many lows. The ability to put forth a winning attitude even when things may not be going your way will set you apart from your less successful counterparts. When the negative mood strikes, resist the temptation to blame the customer, the industry, or the competition; because after all others manage to make things work against the same odds. When the blues come crawling, look within, and take responsibility for freshening up your reserves.

1. During your next sales staff meeting, hand out a sheet of paper to all participants and ask them to nominate all the different things they do to maintain a positive attitude.

2. Once you have compiled the list, choose one activity that you are not doing, and do it for the next week. Each week, add a new item, so that you are always freshening up your repertoire, keeping your attitude positive.

3. Ask your colleagues to monitor your conversations with customers, and offer feedback on alternate ways of handling difficult situations. This will not only shed new light on dark spots, but will build a more collaborative and supportive outlook within your team. Being confident in dealing with tough situations plugs the chinks in your armor where despondency and stress could creep in.

4. Appoint weekly team motivators to be responsible for observing how their team mates are doing and to be cognizant if someone is having a tough day. Team motivators might offer to take a colleague's calls for 15 minutes while they go for a walk or handle an urgent matter. Knowing you have support when you most need it can help to keep you buoyant in stormy seas.

REVIEWING YOUR APPROACH

No salesperson will tell you that he was a star from day one. Getting to the top requires learning and applying the essential skills, and staying at the top means constantly reviewing and updating those skills. There is no greater cause of demotivation than the gradual slide into mediocrity signaled by a continual failure to meet quotas. Constant self-evaluation is a vital weapon in your arsenal against demotivation.

A good way to begin your professional self-evaluation is by taking a look at your daily, weekly, and monthly call reports. Compare the number of cold calls you make to how many appointments you secure, to how many presentations you make, and how many new customers you acquire, as well as the product mix that you have sold, and the base of customers you have maintained and grown.

Be honest with yourself. If you are successful in getting the appointment, but flounder in making the presentation, or have trouble overcoming objections, take action to develop those skills. Strengths and weaknesses will vary throughout your selling profession. I have seen excellent presenters and closers become so smug that they neglect the cold-calling (because with all their presenting and closing success, they would rather not encounter the greater level of rejections associated with cold-calling) and sooner or later find themselves without people to present to.

The best way to make a comprehensive evaluation is to think of all the elements involved in the Consultative Partnership Selling approach using the contents page of this book. Break it down into its constituent parts from Preparing

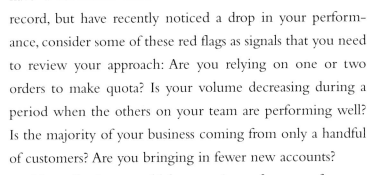

to Sell to Customer Care, and give yourself gradings – excellent, moderate, or poor – based on how well you feel you perform the given task.

If you have been in sales for some time, and have a successful track record, but have recently noticed a drop in your performance, consider some of these red flags as signals that you need to review your approach: Are you relying on one or two orders to make quota? Is your volume decreasing during a period when the others on your team are performing well? Is the majority of your business coming from only a handful of customers? Are you bringing in fewer new accounts?

Naturally there could be a variety of reasons for performance slippage (personal, company-related, burnout, etc.), but if you are still committed to your profession, ask your manager and colleagues for feedback. Perhaps it is time to re-evaluate your strategy as well as your technique. Are you spending a disproportionate amount of time with existing customers and not allocating enough time for prospecting and asking for referrals, perhaps? Look at some of your old call reports from your superstar days and compare your activity levels in the different areas.

Reviewing your approach and technique will help you grow professionally by encouraging you to learn new ways of doing old things and helping you attain new heights.

IMPROVING PERFORMANCE

Once you have reviewed your overall performance, you will be able to make an assessment of your strengths and identify areas for development. Of course the easiest thing is to pat yourself on the back about how brilliant you are, but this will not assist you in becoming even better.

Now you have an idea of areas for improvement, consult some of your trusted colleagues whose opinions and judgment you value. A team-selling approach on some of your calls is an excellent tool that can help you gain valuable insights into your own performance, and watching a colleague at work can suggest new ways of saying and doing things. Some companies hire sales trainers to go out on calls with representatives to evaluate their performance. I do this

on a regular basis for numerous clients, and the salespeople report increased confidence after receiving objective feedback and specific action points for improvement. Of course it is always useful to ask your sales manager to accompany you and help you review your strategy and tactics.

An additional technique that is all too often overlooked but extremely valuable is asking trusted customers to evaluate you as their representative. Ask them what they like about your service and your overall approach to customers. Ask them for an honest account of how you could do better.

The next logical step in improving your performance is deciding on which combination of available resources is best for you. Your company may sponsor a variety of training programs, but what they offer may not fit all your requirements.

If your company is not in a position to sponsor your attendance in external public seminars, perhaps you will decide it is worth your personal investment. Most colleges and universities offer evening extension courses on a variety of topics that may be relevant to you in meeting your personal development goals. Make an Internet search to find out about on-line sales training. Bookstores and libraries are always replenishing their shelves with the latest professional self-help guides. You may also want to consider books on tape if you spend a great deal of time traveling.

By committing yourself to focused life-long learning and personal improvement you will be in a better position to beat demotivation and to creatively and intelligently solve tomorrow's problems.

chapter 5

CUSTOMER CARE AND RETENTION

The Consultative Partnership Selling approach could not be fully realized without its twin component, customer care. As your goal is to build long-lasting relationships with all customers, you will need to be a provider of exceptional customer outreach and support. It all begins with having an attitude toward the customer that clearly communicates, "I value you" and "I'm eager to meet my commitments."

This chapter explores the importance of managing your accounts, and why customer service is essential to your success. We will turn that old approach of dreading complaints into welcoming them, and even viewing them as compliments, which will allow you and your company to grow professionally. We will learn the skills necessary to deal with angry customers and understand how their trust in us can actually increase after they have had a negative experience, if we handle problem-solving skillfully.

The practical steps for building customer relationships and satisfaction and therefore improving overall sales will be outlined in the following pages.

MANAGING ACCOUNTS

During the selling process you painted a picture of your products and services, and created certain expectations in the mind of your prospect. Managing the post-sell process provides you with opportunities to make good on your promises, and even to exceed your client's expectations. Maintaining the satisfaction of your customer could translate into secondary sales and provide you with another testimonial with which to attract new customers.

An old sales adage that I encourage my students to remember is, "Under-promise and over-deliver." At a minimum, always fulfill all the promises you made during the sales process, but also be looking for ways in which you can do more. Be proactive. Check in regularly with your customers, and ask them if there is anything else you can do to insure their continuing satisfaction. Ask if there are problems that need to be solved or questions answered.

Two techniques for making sure your customer always has the service and products that best suit him are "cross-selling" and "up-selling." Cross-selling involves letting your customer know as soon as a new product or service becomes available. Up-selling involves suggesting a suitable upgrade in the product or service when the customer's business changes. Both techniques require you to be in regular contact with the customer, finding out about changes in his company. In this way he will start to see you as a partner who looks after his needs on a continual basis.

WORK SOLUTION 19

Graphing account potential and opportunities

The best way to make sure you are taking care of your accounts is to have a system in place that makes it easy to do so. When you create a document by which to manage the account, and make the client aware you are doing so, the client will feel cared for and appreciated. By charting account potential and opportunities, you greatly minimize the chances of missing them. Whether you are using paper, or creating an electronic graph, here is what you need to do.

1. Based on your account load, determine if you will be creating a single graph for all of your accounts, or a graph for each account you maintain. If you have a customer base with businesses that have multiple locations or numerous sub-accounts, all buying different products from you, then it is a good idea to have a separate graph for each business account.

2. On the vertical axis list the names of your accounts, or if you are creating a separate graph for each account, nominate the primary company and list the sub-accounts.

3. On the horizontal axis list all your company's products/services.

4. Now consider which accounts are taking which products/services. Shade in the squares on the graph where you see you are currently supplying a particular product/service. Unshaded squares denote future account potential.

5. Take the graph with you on each customer visit and review it with your client to ensure they are at all times happy with the products and services they are receiving from you.

CUSTOMER SERVICE

Today's global economy has revolutionized the way people think, behave, and do business. Buyers are becoming more sophisticated and knowledgeable by the minute, and as this trend continues so will their demands and expectations. Our customers have strong opinions about what they want, when they want it, how they want it, and of course all for the lowest possible price. They expect salespeople to be cheerful, and to make them feel special. Why do they behave this way? Because they know they can! If we do not fulfill their needs, they will simply go elsewhere!

It is a business fact of life the competition is always lurking at your customer's door, offering products and services very similar to yours. How do you survive the onslaught? You have worked so hard to sign up your customers, now it is your job to keep them happy and loyal. The best insurance policy against the competitive threat is through the post-sale care and attention you extend to your clients And this is the smartest attitude to have, as it costs five times as much to go out and get a new customer, as it does to hang on to the ones you already have.

As your goal is to maintain your existing customer base as well as to attract new customers, it is critical that you understand customer expectations and perceptions.

A perception is something we hold to be true, based on a direct or indirect experience and/or expectation. Perceived service quality is the difference between what you expect, and what you experience. Here is an example. You go to your favorite restaurant and ask what is the waiting time for a table. You are told 30 minutes. You agree to wait, and your name is called after only 15 minutes. You begin to marvel at how great the service is! Your expectation was 30 minutes, but they called you in 15. As the restaurant exceeded your expectations, your perception of its service is very high. Now you can begin to see the connection between perceptions and expectations.

As you can see you can be very influential in shaping your customers' perceptions. Since your role is to understand your customers in every possible way, it is important that you understand how they come by their expectations. Customers form their opinions and demands based on four primary sources: Advertising; your company's reputation in the marketplace; prior experience with your company; and the level of service extended by your competitors.

The advertising put out by your company informs the marketplace that you exist and creates a certain image in the mind of the buyer. Your reputation is an estimation of how highly regarded you are. Prior experience determines that if we had a good experience with you in the past, we expect the same in the future. The converse of that can be true as well. Your competitors' service and what they are doing in the marketplace also greatly influences customer expectations. If the competition is doing something in a new and improved way, or, for example, offering added services and training, not only will you be expected to do the same, but also your clients will be asking what can you do in addition to that.

In order to better serve your customers and enhance customer retention, you need to fulfill their needs with your product/service and then to dazzle them with your attentive and proactive after-sale service. You will be certain to do this if you use my EMBRACE technique. EMBRACE stands for:

- **Easy** to do business with. Customers want front-line resolution of problems and no hassles.

- **More** than they expect. Remember to under-promise and over-deliver.

- **Bond** with your customers – they are the reason you have a job.

- **Respect** your customers by listening to their needs and concerns and remembering that it is their time and money!

- **Accountability** is demonstrated when you take responsibility for a customer's problem and present a solution.

- **Continuous improvement** is achieved by always

asking the customer and colleagues within our own company, "How can we do better?"

• **Enthusiasm** for your customer is shown when you partner with them by making customer service a priority in your organization and by helping them attain their goals.

Using the EMBRACE method will insure not just a satisfied customer, but also a loyal customer. A satisfied customer is generally pleased with your products and services; but is open to your competitors' offerings. A loyal customer is one that is so dazzled by your company's product and by your after-sale service, that he is far less likely to allow the competition a chance at his business.

When you take care of your customers, they will take care of you by giving you repeat business. Do you adequately EMBRACE your customers?

FLYING THE CUSTOMER-SERVICE FLAG

For the last 12 years I have been traveling internationally conducting my sales, service, and public-speaking seminars, and am a Frequent Traveler with Lufthansa. I feel a particular loyalty to this airline, because year after year they do things right. In light of all the recent airline industry setbacks, they have not skimped on their service. Certainly, to remain competitive they have had to cut back in some areas, but I as the customer do not feel it, because they manage to maintain a superb front-line service. Whenever I fly with Lufthansa, I am warmly greeted at the check-in counter, as I board the plane, and as I exit my flight. The staff is courteous and helpful, and always flexible. It is such service characteristics that keep me accruing miles with this airline, even though from time to time I may find lower fares with its competitors. They have been so reliable, and in turn I am so satisfied, that I would rather not risk experimenting with other carriers. Do you offer the same level of service to your customers?

A COMPLAINT AS A COMPLIMENT

Tension. Fear. Denial. When I was a telecommunications sales representative in Los Angeles, these were some of the emotions that went coursing through my veins whenever I sensed that a customer had a problem with my company's service. The tension, fear, and denial were all alleviated once I received the proper training that made me change my perspective and attitude, and in so doing I gained a real sense of empowerment. I was made to understand that for every customer who actively complains, there are at least 15 to 20 who feel the same way, but do not bother to tell you. Instead they quietly take their business elsewhere. I realized that the complaining customer was actually my friend. Why is this so?

HANDLING COMPLAINTS –
A CASE STUDY

*A few years ago I was a guest at the Ritz Carlton in Maui, Hawaii. I was
very impressed with the level of service I received and observed. Given
that I am an international sales and service trainer, I was curious to
learn about the secrets of their success. I requested an appointment
with a member of management who held the title "Director of Quality."
When we met I was handed a bound booklet entitled Opportunity
Report. The Director told me that the Ritz Carlton's facilities appeal to
the top five percent of discriminating travelers. Competition in this
sector is stiff, and they cannot afford to lose a single one of their
customers to competing chains.*

*As I looked through the Opportunity Report, I realized that it chroni-
cled each and every complaint they received the day before. It included
the name of the customer, his room number, who took the complaint,
and the time it took to resolve it. It also included whatever little
"extra" was extended to the customer as a small compensation for
their inconvenience. The Ritz believes in front-line resolution, and
empowers their employees to exceed the customer's expectations.
They also take care to follow up with the customer to make sure they
are satisfied with the outcome.*

Because he was giving me the opportunity to fix the problem, and that means he believed in me and my company's
product/service. The dissatisfied customer who keeps quiet
because he thinks it would be useless to bring his dissatisfaction to my attention is ripe for the competition's picking!

Learn to think of a complaint as an opportunity.
Customers do not judge us only on how we do things on a
day-to-day basis. They expect us to be working well most of
the time. Their satisfaction with us is based on how we
behave toward them when the service is not working. Were
we fair? Did we take responsibility? Did we fix the problem
or did we fix the blame? A complaint is an opportunity
because very often, after a customer has brought something
to your attention and you have responded, his satisfaction
level actually increases. Now that's a real compliment!

DEALING WITH ANGRY CUSTOMERS

Think back to the last time you had a disappointing customer service experience. Chances are your disappointment had little to do with the product itself. Rather, you felt aggrieved by the attitude of the service provider. There is very little salespeople can do on the spot to change the product, but what they can change is their attitude toward service delivery.

There are behaviors and attitudes that consistently create satisfied customers, and there are those that consistently create customer complaints. Customers respond positively to personalized service, attention to detail, friendliness, caring and sincerity, ownership of problems, responsive solutions, and follow-up. They respond negatively to being passed from

department to department, spoken to in a condescending manner, being reminded of "company policy," and apathy.

When a customer is angry and frustrated, he will not respond to logic until you have given him the opportunity to let off steam. Always remain calm. While the customer is venting, never interrupt him. Let him express himself and finish what he is saying regardless of whether you agree or not. Interrupting him will likely cause him to start repeating himself and only serve to increase his anger. Do, however, let him know you are listening by saying something like, "This is important, I'm writing it down."

Put yourself in the customer's shoes and be empathetic. You can demonstrate your concern and be respectful of the customer's anger by saying something to the effect of, "I'd feel the same way too if this had happened to me" or "I really want to work with you to resolve this, because I know you have a lot better things you can be doing with your time" or "Thank you for your patience, and your feedback. It's because of customers like you that we are able to improve."

Once you have allowed the customer to present his point of view and concerns, paraphrase what you have understood him to say. This accomplishes two things. If you heard the customer correctly, then he will feel listened to and understood, and he will begin to relax. He will feel that progress is being made. If you missed a point or you did not get the message clearly, the customer has the opportunity to put you right. Misunderstanding the issue could lead you to waste time resolving a problem that does not exist.

Once you have dealt adequately with the customer's emotions, you need to move on and tackle the issue. First, thank the customer for bringing the concern to you. Let him know you take responsibility for fixing the problem and will start work on it immediately. Your customer doesn't want to hear excuses, "It's our suppliers' fault" or "No-one told me" or "I'm new here." It is your company and the customer expects you to do all the running around until you can get to the bottom of the problem. The more people he needs to talk to within your organization to resolve his problem, the lower his opinion of your service.

Your customer expects quick resolution of his problem, and often likes to be involved in deciding the outcome, so give him options. This gives him a feeling of having more control over his situation. Much of a customer's irritation with service-related issues stems from a sense of helplessness. Get into the habit of telling them what you can do for them, instead of what cannot be done. "We can do this, this, or this. Which is best for you, Mr. Jones?"

Once you have resolved a customer's issue to his satisfaction, ask him what else you can do for him. Always follow up with your customer the following day to make sure all is well, and try to do something extra for him to recognize the fact that he has been inconvenienced (for example, a thank you note, phone call, or company promotional gift).

Remember that the worst thing you can do is ignore a person's anger. If you wish to maintain his business, hear him out, take responsibility, give him options and follow up.

WORK SOLUTION 20

Creating memorable customer experiences

Ensuring superb customer service means you place a value on what is important to the customer, and it shows. When you exceed customer expectations, you contribute to a sense of harmony and well-being not only for the customer, but also for yourself. Customers who are well served remain loyal and ultimately make our lives easier. The following exercise helps us keep this principle at the forefront of our minds.

1. For five consecutive business days keep a list of customer complaints.

2. Categorize them: Which relate to the product itself and which relate to some aspect of your service delivery, such as keeping promises, employee attitude, etc.

3. In each situation directly relating to service delivery, ask yourself how the situation could have been turned around. Keep in mind that, although you may not be able to remedy every situation on the spot, making a visible effort on behalf of the customer will often suffice.

4. Develop good service habits one by one. By examining the list you created in Step 2, pick the most glaring less-than-excellent thing you do, and replace it with a more customer-oriented one. Track your successes as they develop.

5. Think of an occasion when you as a customer experienced what you would describe as extraordinary treatment. List the characteristics of the experience. What did people say or do that was memorable?

6. Keep the answer to the following question in your mind: Why is providing extraordinary customer service a benefit to you as well as the customer?

QUALITY AS YOUR SALES AND SERVICE EDGE

In today's competitive environment, it is not too difficult for one company to match another's prices, sales, and promotions. It is a great challenge, however, to offer superior service. The best way to distinguish your product/service from that of competitors is to offer quality in your service standard, and your attitude needs to reflect this.

In recent years organizations worldwide have taken this approach to heart by adopting the standards of Dr. W. Edwards Deming who revolutionized quality standards with a method known as TQM, Total Quality Management. This is a system of management processes designed actively to exceed customer expectations. The Deming TQM approach

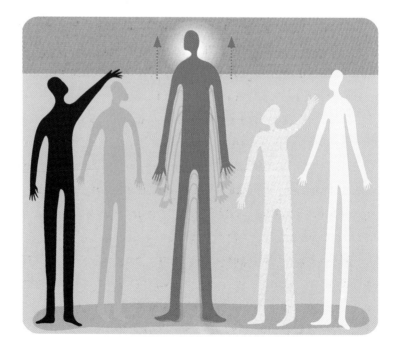

stresses the significance of modeling your business values around customer needs and wants, and includes some of the following precepts.

Move away from being price driven. Focus on building value in the eyes of your customers by selling service and quality. This is the key to building long-term partnerships.

Case in point: While conducting a customer-service seminar in Moscow for a leading telecommunications provider, I felt it was important for the customer-service representatives to hear first hand what their customers valued. CNN was a major customer, so I invited the Bureau Chief to speak to the group. He applauded the efforts and talents of the service team by telling them the following: "As a media organization I use not only the services of your company, but those of your two major competitors as well. If I had the luxury, I'd toss the other two out, and use only your company." The service reps were startled, because their company was twice as expensive as the other two major players. He continued, "Yours is the only company that is responsive whenever I have a service issue. You take responsibility, you follow up, and do something extra. You never make excuses. That's a service that's a better value to me."

Make your company the benchmark. Determine the quality of your sales and service endeavors based on customer satisfaction. Strive to be your industry leader – the company that your competitors look to as a "standard setter."

Think about the companies you love to do business with. What is it about their service that makes you enjoy being their customer? Do you feel valued? Are they reliable? Do they pay attention to detail?

Understand your internal market. Realize that all the departments within your company depend on one another to provide seamless, high-quality service. How well individuals within your company (internal customers) are linked and served, directly affect those who pay for your goods and services (external customers).

Case in point: In numerous cases, I have seen sales organizations make special concessions for customers, only to fail adequately to communicate those concessions to the technical department, order fulfillment, or accounting. In some cases, the concessions were communicated internally, but there was inadequate follow-up. This would result in enormous customer dissatisfaction, and all of the value, rapport, and expectations that had been fixed in his mind, would be radically diminished. Do not shoot yourself in the foot. Coordinate effectively with other departments.

Be responsive to customer feedback. Whenever customers express dissatisfaction, take action. If you do things right, the relationship could be even stronger after the complaint was received because you have had the opportunity to demonstrate your "pro-service" attitude.

Case in point: I was recently visiting my favorite aunt Ankica in Zagreb, Croatia, and when we sat down to breakfast, we realized that the long-life milk we had just opened had a very bad taste. My aunt was prepared just to throw it out, and never purchase that brand again. I noticed on the milk carton there was a toll-free number for customer feedback. I urged her to call it, but she was reluctant. I persisted. I told her the company needed to know. She called and the service representative was very efficient, friendly, and responsible. He asked for her address and within 30 minutes an employee appeared at her door with a basket full of products: luncheon meats, cheese, replacement milk, yogurt! My aunt was amazed. Two hours later a supervisor called and thanked her for reporting the incident, and for being their customer. My aunt was talking about it for weeks. She told her friends what a great company they were, and now has a higher than ever opinion of them. See the impact of not letting a single customer slip away?

Many companies realize the importance of product quality, but forget about service quality. However, companies that start to focus on service see a marked improvement in sales results. As sales-force expenses typically account for a major part of budget expenditure, service enhancements will translate into improved sales quality! This means valuable bottom line benefits for the business as a whole.

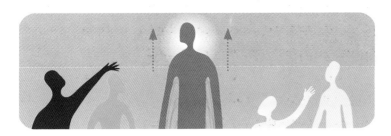

EXCEEDING CUSTOMER EXPECTATIONS

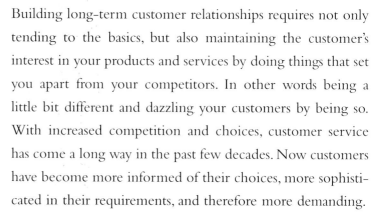

Building long-term customer relationships requires not only tending to the basics, but also maintaining the customer's interest in your products and services by doing things that set you apart from your competitors. In other words being a little bit different and dazzling your customers by being so. With increased competition and choices, customer service has come a long way in the past few decades. Now customers have become more informed of their choices, more sophisticated in their requirements, and therefore more demanding.

Increased competition and customer demands is the very essence of what has made our work life so much more stressful; but if we know what to expect and acquire some of the necessary tools, we can minimize the negative effects of stress. So what do we need to keep in mind to provide exceptional customer service and exceed our customer expectations?

In my customer-service seminars, I talk about the importance of two terms I call "Core Links," and "Differentiation

DISAPPEARING DIFFERENTIALS

Several years ago a well-known American department store started to offer its customers the services of a personal shopper to do their clothes shopping for them. And they introduced price adjustments, whereby if an item already purchased went on sale two weeks after it was bought, the customer could bring in her receipt and ask to be refunded the difference between the regular and the sale price. At the time these were wonderful innovations that marked the store out from its competitors. Today they are standard in American retailing. The best way to exceed your customers' expectations is by doing the unexpected on a continual basis, and to keep asking your customers "What else can we do to make our product/service better, and how can we improve our service delivery?"

Links." Core links comprise your basic service offering. In the business sector it is whatever could be considered a constant among you and your competitors, the standard fare which you all offer. This could be the hours of operation, your pricing schedule, rate of service delivery, and so on. Differentiation Links are the things you do that set you apart from your competitors. For example, the Lexus dealership where I take my car to be serviced provides me with a loaner car to use while my car is being serviced. They also serve fresh pastries, coffee, and tea, and have a self-serve soda bar. They not only have a very comfortable and clean waiting area, they provide private work cubicles where you can place phone calls, or hook up your laptop and work until your car is ready. To top it all off, every car they service is cleaned and vacuumed. These Differentiation Links mean that I will not be looking for an alternative servicing option in the next few years.

The interesting thing behind Differentiation Links is that before you know it, your competitors will be imitating you, and before long, the "extras" that you are providing will intertwine, and become part of the service standard. What differentiated you from your competitors is now expected by all customers from all suppliers. Then you will need to confer with your colleagues and customers and ask, "What new steps can we take to stand out?"

MAINTAINING CUSTOMER LOYALTY

Today more than ever retaining customers requires as much attention as every other step in the sales process. So what are proven ways to enhance customer retention?

First, stay in touch. Failing to follow up with your customers and maintain contact is a form of self-sabotage. You can be certain your competitors will be calling and the surest way to lock them out is to keep a close, mutually beneficial relationship with your clients. As your customer's consultant and partner, you are also in essence a part of his company. He is relying on you to be updating his product and service offering whenever it benefits him. For this reason it is important that you tell him that you view this as your commitment

to him and that you will be in touch via e-mail, phone calls, newsletters, luncheons, and meetings. Remember it is much more difficult for a customer to leave someone with whom he has a relationship than a stranger.

Make every effort to ensure you are always responsive to your customer's concerns and problems. Remember that a lost customer is never confined to just one sale or just one person. A dissatisfied customer is statistically likely to tell between 11 and 16 others, and has the potential to exaggerate the story each time. Research shows that if customers feel you are responsive to a problem, they will do business with you again in 82 to 95 percent of cases.

Make every effort to ensure that the only surprise your customers receive from you is how well you exceed their expectations! In the same way minimize "negative surprises," simply by being realistic and honest. I made it a policy to share with my customers information about the most common occasional "set-backs" they may experience. We would agree on what we would do should such circumstances arise. I also made sure they knew who to contact if I were absent. This did not detract from my relationship with the customer. In fact, the result was completely the opposite. The client appreciated my honesty as part of a trusting relationship and was happy to feel equipped to deal with possible problems.

Keeping your promises, staying in touch, and keeping the client informed are sure ways to boost customer loyalty. Being flexible, responsive, and respectful will keep them happy members of your business family.

FURTHER READING

Connor, T., *Soft Sell,* Sourcebooks (Naperville, Illinois), 2003

Covey, S. R., *Seven Habits of Highly Effective People,* Free Press (New York), 1989

Duncan, T., *High Trust Selling,* Thomas Nelson Publishers (Nashville, Tennessee), 2002

Farber, Barry J., *Sales Secrets From Your Customers,* Career Press (Franklin Lakes, New Jersey), 1995

Harrell, K., *Attitude is Everything,* Harper Business Books (New York), 2003

Harvard Business Essentials, *Negotiation,* Harvard Business School Press (Cambridge, MA), 2003

Heiman, S., Sanchez, D., & Tuleja, T., *The New Conceptual Selling,* Warner Books (New York), 1999

LeBoeuf, M., *How to Win Customers and Keep Them for Life,* Berkley Publishing (New York), 2000

Mitchell, J., *Hug Your Customers,* Hyperion (New York), 2003

Smith, B. & Rutgliano, T., *Discover Your Sales Strengths,* Warner Books (New York), 2003

Willingham, R. *Integrity Selling for the 21st Century,* Doubleday (New York), 2003

INDEX

INDEX **155**

User Groups 17
see also prospects
cuttings services 16

D
data *see* information
databases 26
decision making *see*
  purchasing decisions
Deming, W. Edwards 146–7
demonstrations 93
design 23
diagrams 23, 92
dialogue *see* communication
Differentiation Links 150–51
directories 26
drama 93
dress 32, 64–5

E
EMBRACE technique 138–9
employers, relationships with
  13
energy 114–15, 121–2
enthusiasm 35–6
equipment 95
estimating 19
evaluation *see* qualifying *and*
  self-evaluation
excuses 144, 147
expectations and perceptions
  134, 136–9, 153
extras 150–51
  see also service
eye-contact 49, 51, 66, 67, 78

F
facial expression 32, 65
fact finding 58–61, 87
fear *see* anxiety

feedback 15, 130–31
  responding to 148–9
  see also
    concerns/objections *and*
    restatement
financial considerations *see*
  price
follow-up 21, 85
  see also service
forecasting 19
formality 49

G
gestures 65–6
gifts 144
goals 13, 25, 77, 116–19, 147
  personal 77, 116–19,
    128–31
  see also objectives
  and quotas
graphics 23, 92
graphs 23, 92, 135
grooming 64
group decision-making 96–9

H
honesty 153
humor 35, 93

I
ice-breaking 51
image 23
  listening and 79
  see also appearance *and*
    speech
Immediate Benefits Statement
  56–7, 82
industry organizations 16, 24
informality 49
information 39, 58–61

sources of 16
  see also qualifying
information/knowledge
  management 20, 21
intentions *see* goals
Internet 16, 26, 131
introductions 96–7
investment recovery 84, 87

K
kindness, random 125–6
knowledge *see* information

L
language 68–9
  see also wording
leads and lead-generation 21,
  26–9
  see also cold calling
learning 124–5, 131
listening 46, 49–50, 76–9,
  86–7
    making connections
      during 91–2
    to objections 103
lists 26
lose/win outcomes 104–7
loyalty *see* relationships *under*
  customers

M
market knowledge 16
market research 16
measurement
  of activity/performance
    18–19, 24, 25, 128–31
  of objectives/goals 40, 41,
    117
meetings 50
  sales teams 24, 127

V

value and value-added 84–5, 87, 101
   see also benefits
values 116, 119
   see also goals
verbal buying signals 109–11
visual aids 23, 92–4
visual communication 92
   see also non-verbal communication
visual image *see* image
vocals 69–71
   observing 78
   relative importance 92

W

wants *see under* needs
websites *see* Internet
win/lose outcomes 104–7
wording 68–9
   examples 36, 45, 57, 61, 63, 86–7, 99, 110, 143, 144
   relative importance 92
   on slides 92

ACKNOWLEDGMENTS

A very special thanks to the talented editorial staff at Duncan Baird Publishers – Judy Barratt, Julia Charles, and Louise Bostock – and to illustrators Melvyn Evans and Ken Orvidas.

Thank you to all of the following significant others for your assistance and guidance:

Teta Ankica Butigan, Dr. Thomas Cook, Paul Falchi, Leszek Izdebski, Cindy Javelet, Teresa & Spyros Kalantzis, Stanko Lovric, Cristina Molteni, Sharon Mullagh, Darrell Norris, Margaret Von Treskow, Tata Yanko, Nick & John Susac, and to my favorite teachers from childhood and young adulthood, who always motivated me with their support and enthusiasm: Mrs. Gigi Pack, Mrs. Geraldine Baskerville, Dr. Barbara O'Connor, Mary Daugherty, and Mrs. Sylvia Wessel.

If you would like to offer suggestions for other ways of forming consultative partnerships with clients or share your experiences of creating mutually beneficial relationships in the selling situation, or if you or your organization would like further information about my work with sales teams and organizations, I would be very pleased if you would contact me – kristina@strategictraining.net – or see our website at www.strategictraining.net.